Nothing But Net

Business the Cisco Way

DAVID STAUFFER

CAPSTONE

Copyright © David Stauffer 2000

The right of David Stauffer to be indentified as the author of this work has been asserted in accordance with the Copyright, Designs and Patents Act 1988

First published 2000 by
Capstone Publishing Inc.
40 Commerce Park
Milford
CT 06460
USA
Contact: info@capstonepub.com

Capstone Publishing Ltd
Oxford Centre for Innovation
Mill Street
Oxford OX2 0JX
United Kingdom
http://www.capstone.co.uk

British Library Cataloguing in Publication Data
A CIP catalogue record for this book is available from the British Library

US Library of Congress Cataloging-in-Publication Data
Library of Congress Card Number: 00-103175

ISBN 1-84112-087-1

Typeset by Forewords, Oxford, UK
Printed and bound in the USA by
Sheridan Books, Ann Arbor, Michigan

This book is printed on acid-free paper

Substantial discounts on bulk quantities of Capstone books are available to corporations, professional associations and other organizations. If you are in the USA or Canada, phone the LPC Group, Special Sales Department for details on 1 800 626 4330, or fax 1 800 243 0138. Everywhere else, phone Capstone Publishing on +44 1865 811113, or fax +44 1865 240941.

CONTENTS

PREFACE

Do you want to make your organization more successful by learning from another company's spectacular success? If so, you probably can do no better than looking at Cisco Systems, the company that drives the Internet. For many reasons, Cisco appears to be the right company . . . in the right business . . . at the right time.

THE RIGHT COMPANY . . .

Cisco went public at the dawn of the 1990s (16 February 1990). During the ensuing decade, its stock price appreciated by 82,300 percent – placing it at the top of the heap among all US stocks, with the likes of America Online and Dell Computer, for percentage gain in the 1990s. If you bought $10,000 of Cisco stock at the IPO price, it was worth $8.2 million at the turn of the millennium.[1]

Cisco is thought to be the fastest-growing firm in world history, reaching market capitalization of $100 billion in only 12 years.[2] Microsoft made it to that level in 20 years. Cisco's market cap, since passing the century mark, more than doubled in another two years, to make the company the fifth-biggest in the world at the dawn of the new millennium.

CISCO'S SOARING STOCK VALUE

Cisco's Investor Relations Department reports the calendar year-end value of the company's stock for the 1990s as follows. Prices for 1990 through 1998 have been adjusted for stock splits to reflect values in relation to year-end 1999.

Year-end	Share price ($)	Year's % increase	% increase over IPO (16 Feb 1990)
1990	0.31	138	138
1991	0.92	197	608
1992	2.19	138	1,585
1993	3.59	64	2,662
1994	3.91	9	2,908
1995	8.30	112	6,285
1996	14.14	70	10,777
1997	18.58	31	14,192
1998	46.41	150	35,600
1999	107.12	131	82,300

As for the CEO, since ascending to Cisco's top post, John Chambers has guided the company from $1.3 billion in revenues in 1994 to $12.2 billion only five years later.[3] He is widely acknowledged as the reigning king of acquisitions, having gobbled up other firms at the rate of nine per year since becoming CEO. And he's compiled his impressive financial scorecard without the sort of human relations carnage associated with the likes of "Chainsaw" Al Dunlap – winning praise from within and outside the company for scuttling top management perks, being respectful and frank with employees, and thus winning an astounding worker retention rate.

. . . IN THE RIGHT BUSINESS . . .

In a now-annual study commissioned by Cisco, researchers at the University of Texas' Center for Research in Electronic Commerce found that the so-called Internet economy "grew 68 percent from the first quarter of 1998 to the first quarter of 1999 and now accounts for 2.3 million jobs."

The study found that in 1999 the Internet economy would grow to $507 billion, versus $301 billion in 1998. That makes Internet business bigger than such long-established key US industries as telecommunications ($300 billion) and airlines ($355 billion), and positions it to overtake publishing ($750 billion) and – sometime around 2003 to 2005, the gargantuan healthcare industry ($1 trillion).

> Your $10,000 invested in Cisco at the 1990 IPO price had grown to $6.5 million at the turn of the millennium.

Online sales, a sector of the Internet economy, increased 127 percent to $37.5 billion from the first quarter of 1998 to the first quarter of 1999. For the same periods, the number of jobs dedicated to online sales increased to 900,882, a 78 percent increase. Other sectors registered less dramatic growth, but no gain was less than 50 percent.

The number of companies participating in the Internet economy has also surged. One in three of the 3,400 companies surveyed for the most recent University of Texas report didn't exist before 1996. The study also found that 2,000 new secure websites are added every month, "reflecting the creation of new companies and shifting of existing businesses to the Internet."

One of three companies surveyed in the 1999 Internet economy study didn't exist before 1996.

Beyond the Texas study, more numbers attest to the rocketing role of the Internet in the US and world economies. For example, the US Department of Commerce says that in 1993, 3 million Americans were connected to the Net and there were 26,000 domain names in use. By 1999, corresponding numbers had jumped to 80 million connected Americans and 5 million websites.[4]

What each of these gee-whiz growth numbers means to networking market leader Cisco, of course, is more customers, and more orders, more "Submit" mouse clicks on their cash-cow website that already handles orders worth $32 million every day.

. . . AT THE RIGHT TIME

With all due credit to the company and its current CEO, Cisco and Chambers couldn't have timed their presence and ascent in the data networking business better if they'd had a dead-on-target crystal ball. *New York Times* columnist Thomas L. Friedman observed that over the three years from 1995 to 1998, the best single measure of power in the global economy shifted from personal computers per household (preferred, understandably, by Microsoft) to "networks per capita" (so nominated by Silicon Valley's "cutting-edge technology companies"). According to Friedman, "Bandwidth and degree of connectivity – those are the new measures of power in the Silicon Universe." [5]

Chambers himself frequently acknowledges that timing is a considerable contributor to Cisco's success, as when he told a cable TV news anchor that Internet gear-making is "the right industry to be in at the right time."[6]

SO WHAT, EXACTLY, MAKES THE ECONOMY NEW?[7]

Folks from prime ministers and presidents to twenty-something Silicon Valley CEOs talk about the "new economy," though none ever seem to say what it is. Someone who has is Randolph Court of the Progressive Policy Institute, a Washington, DC, think tank. He lists four defining characteristics of the new economy:

◆ *Knowledge* – is prized above muscle, manpower, and even know-how in the form of experience.

◆ *Globalization* – means you'll find your customers, suppliers, partners, and employees just about anywhere on earth. A firm's factory – if it even has any – is as likely to be in Malaysia or Mexico as in the building behind headquarters. And that factory, no matter where it is, probably gets raw materials or parts from other countries.

◆ *Competition* – is all-pervasive and unrelenting. New products and services are developed faster and new companies are being started at a pace never experienced before. Startups, innovating like there's no tomorrow (for many, there isn't), seem poised by the thousands to overthrow any corporate behemoth that lets down its guard for more than a day.

◆ *Information* – is being mined and moved at light speed in prodigious quantities, transforming the way companies do business and how people work.

. . . AND MAKING THE MOST OF GOOD FORTUNE

So Cisco has benefitted considerably from both internal and external conditions that have aided the firm's spectacular growth and profitability. But it would be a mistake to view those conditions as anything more than assists – agents that contributed only to an ambient environment in which Cisco's leaders have repeatedly made smart decisions that have carried the company to the top.

"Good fortune and good timing may have given Cisco a solid start," London's *Financial Times* observes. "But the company's remarkable growth record is largely the result of astute management." Analyst Amar Senan of Volpe, Welty & Co. notes that "IBM was slow to realize the impact of personal computers on its mainframe business," while "Cisco readily embraced switching" when switches were emerging as an alternative to the routers that were once virtually the sole product Cisco offered. The *FT* says Cisco has similarly "been swift to adapt to new trends in the quickly changing field of networking technology."[8]

> **"[Cisco's] remarkable growth record is largely the result of astute management."**
> **– Financial Times**

There is much for any manager or entrepreneur to learn from such an outfit. Read on to know how Cisco has capitalized on opportunities like no company before.

Author's note

Cisco declined my requests to have a corporate voice in the pages of this book. (The head of Cisco PR told me that John Chambers has found that CEOs often seem to get interested in books extolling their success shortly before their companies' performance heads south.) Nonetheless, my research was greatly aided by folks in Cisco public relations and investor relations who responded to my specific inquiries regarding the company's history and financial results. I appreciate their efforts.

NOTES

1. Cisco Investor Relations Department compilation for author; Browning, E.S., "Goodbye Golden Decade. Now What Will the '00s Bring?," *Wall Street Journal*, 13 December 1999; and Pender, Kathleen, "A Boom–Bust Year for IPOs," *San Francisco Chronicle*, 8 January 1991.

2. Gomes, Lee, "Cisco Tops $100 Billion in Market Capital," *Wall Street Journal*, 20 July 1998.

3. Reinhardt, Andy, "The Man Who Hones Cisco's Cutting Edge," *Business Week*, 13 September 1999.

4. Internet Indicators Website: www.internetindicators.com.

5. Friedman, Thomas L., "The Internet Wars," *New York Times*, 11 April 1998.

6. CNNfn Network, "Street Sweep," 16 November 1999.

7. Boulton, Guy, "What's New About the Economy," *Salt Lake Tribune*, 31 October 1999.

8. Kehoe, Louise, "Providing the Plumbing for the Internet," *Financial Times*, 14 May 1996.

Introduction

CISCO: THE COMPANY THAT'S BEEN WHERE YOURS IS GOING

66 T he Internet will change everything," says Cisco Systems CEO John Chambers, reflecting the thinking of many experts who assess the impact of emerging information technology on business.[1]

Chambers may or may not be literally correct about the impact of the Internet, but events leading up to the dawn of a new millennium leave no doubt that new technologies, new realities of commerce and competition, and the blinding pace of change have combined to fundamentally alter business and business management forever.

Cisco's corporate advertising asks the key question raised by emergence of the "new world" way of working: "Are you ready?" To which almost anyone's honest answer, given that change today is continuous, must be no.

> **"If you wait for the revolution to happen, then most likely you will be overthrown."**
> **– John Chambers**

But almost any manager can be better prepared by taking a close look at secrets of the rise of Cisco Systems. The reason can be found in the words of *Fortune* magazine reporter Brent Schlender:

> The reality is that the Internet, for all its buzz, has wrought flashy but mainly superficial change in most industries so far. . . . What we've seen up to now is just an overture: It will take years for this saga to play itself out. One big industry, however,

is already feeling the full force of how profoundly disruptive the Internet can be. It's the one that brought us the Internet in the first place. . . . It's a collection of substantial businesses whose very real products soak up about 50 percent of the capital spending of American private enterprise.

And among the substantial companies in the world of Internet networking, Schlender writes, "the granddaddy of them all is Cisco Systems."[2]

Cisco is a super-successful company that's already been where just about every business on earth is headed. To know Cisco's secrets – to understand what the company has faced, how it has responded, and how its moves have worked out – is to know something about what may well lay ahead for every enterprise. John Chambers knows why that's important: "If you see it coming ahead of time, you can position yourself," he says. "But if you wait for the revolution to happen, then most likely you will be overthrown."[3]

CISCO IN A NUTSHELL[4]

Founded: 1984, by Leonard Bosack and Sandy Lerner, husband and wife and Stanford University academics, who devised a way to send data between their separate computers. When colleagues wanted "routers," too, and Stanford said no to an internal enterprise, the couple left to build them at home.

First sale: In 1986, a router assembled in the founders' kitchen, living room, or garage – depending on whose account you choose to believe.

IPO: 16 February 1990.

Primary business: The routers, switches, and other data networking gear, plus associated software and services, that are often described as the "plumbing" or "guts" of the Internet.

Headquarters: San Jose, California, with major operations in Research Triangle Park, North Carolina, and Chelmsford, Massachusetts.

Employees: 21,000 total; 10,000 in San Francisco Bay Area.

Annual revenues: $12.2 billion in 1999, an increase of 17,600% over the $69 million earned in 1990.

Named after: A small California town in the Sierra Nevada Mountains.

Current corporate slogan: "Empowering the Internet generation."

Current image advertising tagline: "Are you ready?"

Senior management:
  John Chambers, President & CEO
  Larry Carter, Chief Financial Officer
  Don Listwin, Executive Vice President
  Judy Estrin, Chief Technical Officer
  Gary Daichendt, Executive Vice President, Worldwide Operations

Websites: www.cisco.com and a Cisco-sponsored offshoot: www.internetindicators.com

WHY CISCO IS A GREAT CASE STUDY

The secrets of success for Cisco are well worth studying on the basis of the company's spectacular financial performance and its leading-edge response to a new world of continuous change. Those are reasons enough to take a look at Cisco, but others make the company an even more valuable object of close examination:

◆ For an Internet-related company, Cisco has a track record.

Yes, it's less than 20 years old, but that's at least long enough to track strategies and decisions over time and see how they've turned out.

◆ Cisco is perhaps as close as Silicon Valley can come to a company that largely sells tangible, space-occupying products. A router is a physical object that's composed of parts, assembled, shipped, and installed – a process not associated with the typical dot-com firm or many other companies composing the Internet economy. That can provide a measure of familiarity for the manager who would like to learn from successful Internet firms, but has a hard time identifying with the purely intangible offerings of a company like Yahoo.

◆ Unlike many other high-tech firms with stratospheric market capitalizations, Cisco actually accomplishes – spectacularly – one of the key objectives of any company: profitability. Cisco's valuation is based to a considerable degree on past performance and realistic projections of future performance, rather than on pie-in-the-sky expectations.

◆ The company soared to success in relative obscurity and totally without the media hype that some experts believe accounts for astronomical valuations of other Internet firms. As recently as 1998, *New York Times* columnist Thomas L. Friedman called Cisco "the most important American company that no one has ever heard of."[5]

◆ Cisco has more experience than most companies in using some of the currently hottest competitive tools, such as strategic partnering, outsourcing, and configuring a virtual supply chain.

◆ At the same time, Cisco practices that old time religion, emphasizing tried and true corporate virtues such as superb customer service and employee relations.

> "Cisco Systems' [Web]site practically defines effective business-to-business Internet marketing." – *Business Marketing*

◆ Cisco is the acknowledged champion of business-to-business e-commerce selling, with a website that rings up an average $32 million in sales every day. "Most companies these days are sticking a toe in the electronic commerce waters," reports *Business Marketing* magazine. "Some have even decided to wade right in. And then there's a company that's in right up to its neck and swimming fast enough to win the top spot on Net-Marketing's [1999] list of the top 200 business-to-business Websites. Cisco Systems' site practically defines effective business-to-business Internet marketing."[6]

JOHN CHAMBERS: THE UN-SILICON EVERYMAN

The story of Cisco's stunning, world-beating growth is inseparable from the story of CEO John Chambers. He's worthy of careful examination for reasons in addition to the spectacularly on-target moves he's made as Cisco's top manager:

◆ He comes across as a regular guy. Few written descriptions of Chambers fail to mention his unassuming, aw-shucks de-

JOHN CHAMBERS' HALF-CENTURY[7]

Born: 23 August 1949, Cleveland, Ohio.

Early years: Reared in Charleston, West Virginia, the only son of two doctors. His father was a part-time entrepreneur, owning a motel and restaurant.

School: Did poorly until dyslexia was diagnosed and parents responded by hiring a tutor. Earned bachelor's and law degree at West Virginia University and an MBA from Indiana University in 1975.

Employment: In sales at IBM for six years, followed by eight years at Wang in senior sales management. Joined Cisco in 1991 as number two to John Morgridge; named CEO in 1995 when Morgridge relinquished the post, as planned, to serve as chairman.

Family: Married to Elaine Prater more than 25 years; one son, one daughter.

Diversions: Jogging, tennis, fishing.

Dislike: Reading in any form, for business or pleasure, owing to the dyslexia that plagued him as a child and still causes discomfort today.

meanor or his easy-going, twangy, West Virginia drawl – characteristics that stand in sharp contrast to the hyperactive, helium-voice presentation more typically associated with high-tech sector CEOs.

◆ Bits and bytes aren't in his blood. Although he's worked only for technology firms (IBM, Wang, and Cisco), Chambers – perhaps unlike any other high-tech CEO – earned degrees in law and business and rose through the ranks in sales and sales management.[8]

◆ His business background is more similar than that of other Silicon Valley CEOs to the career experiences of most managers. "Of the [high-tech] industry's most successful companies, there's only one – Cisco – that has been run for a long time by a conventional professional CEO," writes Vermeer Technologies founder Charles H. Ferguson, in his book *High Stakes, No Prisoners*. "Intel, Microsoft, Oracle, AOL, Compaq, Dell, and Gateway are all run by founders, early employees, and/or former academics."[9]

> "Of the [high-tech] industry's most successful companies, there's only one – Cisco – that has been run for a long time by a conventional professional CEO." – Vermeer Technologies founder Charles H. Ferguson

◆ In the same vein, Chambers is of a more traditional and common age for a big-company CEO – about two decades older than many of the brilliant, Stanford-educated digitheads who run other Silicon Valley startups.

◆ He does the hard work of managing without fanfare. Where more renowned CEOs such as Jack Welch have catchy names such as Work-Out and Six Sigma attached to their performance improvement initiatives, Chambers sticks consistently to the proven and reliable – if unexciting – fundamentals.

CHAMBERS' FOUR SIMPLE STEPS TO SUCCESS[10]

John Chambers is a practical and direct corporate leader, as he illustrates in providing this list of steps to business success in the book *Lessons From the Top*, by executive recruiters Thomas J. Neff and James M. Citrin:

1. Within reason, you can accomplish almost anything in life that you want to, as long as you're willing to work hard – and smart – to get it.

2. Deal with life the way it is, not the way you wish it was.

3. Treat people the way you would like to be treated yourself.

4. Have fun. Don't take life too seriously.

HOW CISCO – AND CHAMBERS – PUT IT ALL TOGETHER

The stories of Cisco and Chambers have been recounted and analyzed and dissected in veritable mountains of articles, books, and analysts' reports. From these many sources and viewpoints, 10 secrets of Cisco's success emerge:

1. Make Your Passion Your Business – Preach It Always Everywhere. Chambers seems genuinely to act first in the interest of a cause, secondarily in the interest of revenue and profits. The cause, he never tires of saying, is to extend the Internet – the greatest educational and poverty-fighting tool in human history – to every corner of the globe.

2. Win the World with E-commerce. Cisco's powerhouse website pulls in $32 million in sales daily, accounting for 80 percent of the company's total revenue. About half of these orders go directly to subcontractors that manufacture, test, and ship the equipment direct to the customer; the first involvement of a Cisco employee is handling the customer's check. Some 70 percent of customer-support calls are handled over the Internet, again, with no real-time involvement of a Cisco employee.

3. Use the Net to Revolutionize Internal Operations. Cisco further leverages the power of the Net to streamline internal operations. Example: The company's "virtual" close of quarterly books follows the calendar date of close by only 24 hours. A variety of human resources functions – most prominently, staff recruiting – are almost entirely Internet based, and the company is in the midst of shifting its training to the Net.

4. Put People Before Products, Profits, and Everything Else. Chambers is known for valuing employees above products, services, systems, and programs. One result: employee attrition in Cisco-acquired companies is dramatically lower than the industry average. Pay and empowerment are key Chambers tools, along with innovative accents such as "birthday breakfasts," where employees are invited during the month of their birthdays to grill the CEO on any Cisco matter.

5. Listen Constantly to Customers. Chambers listens to his field managers' voice-mail reports on Cisco's biggest customers every evening of every day of the year. He has been late for meetings with his own board and even a head of state because he was on the phone with a customer. His "obsessive" concern for the customer even extends to buyouts: Cisco has made two acquisitions first suggested by customers.

6. Serve Your Core Customers from Start to End-to-End. Cisco aims to satisfy every networking need of its customers, which means developing or acquiring every related new technology that comes down the pike. Chambers boasts that Cisco's "horizontal" business model – which in practice links a far-reaching network of suppliers, customers, and strategic partners – is the only way to meet customers' ever-changing needs.

7. Look to Lead in Every Line of Business. Cisco aims to be number one or two in market share in every one of its products and services. That goal has been met in 20 lines of Cisco business. But now the battlefield has widened to include the "converged" transmission of data, voice, and video, where Cisco is a market-share David, going up against Goliaths such as Lucent and Nortel in a showdown for 21st century dominance.

8. Buy Right to Grow Like Gangbusters. Chambers believes that any company that's not among the first five to introduce a new technology will only catch up by acquiring one of the five that did. Thus, Cisco has bought forty-something companies since 1993, and a division of 60 employees is constantly evaluating potential new targets.

9. If You Don't Buy 'Em, Join 'Em. Leading-edge companies regularly enter strategic alliances when they offer strong mutual benefits and a route to market leadership – some firms maintain thousands of such relationships at once. Partnering is increasingly a necessity, not an option, for successfully competing in an ever-changing world, and Cisco does it as well as anyone.

10. Resist Complacency That Can Accompany Success. Chambers is happily uncomforted by Cisco's fabulous success

---

CISCO'S CORPORATE TIME LINE[11]

◆ 1984
Founded by Leonard Bosack and Sandy Lerner when their employer, Stanford University, didn't allow them to build and install routers for colleagues.

◆ 1986
Ships its first product, an AGS router.

◆ 1987
Succeeds after 76 turn-downs in securing its first and only venture capital funding, from Sequoia Capital. Sequoia partner Donald T. Valentine becomes Cisco's chairman.
Hires tenth employee.

◆ 1988
Bosack and Lerner, under pressure from Valentine and other board members, sell their interests for $174 million.
Valentine hires John Morgridge as president and CEO.

◆ 1989
Hires 100th employee.

◆ 1990
Goes public with IPO on February 16.
World Wide Web is launched.

◆ 1991
John Chambers is hired as executive VP.
Surpasses $100 million annual revenue.

◆ 1992
Publishes first advertisement.

◆ 1993
Expands beyond routers as a supplier of "end-to-end" network solutions.
Makes first acquisition: Crescendo Communications.
Hires 1000th employee.

◆ 1994
Surpasses $1 billion annual revenue.
Launches Web and e-commerce site: Cisco Connection Online.
Acquires three companies (total to date = 4).

◆ 1995
Leadership dominoes (all by mutual consent): Chambers named president and CEO, Morgridge becomes chairman, Valentine vice chairman.
Acquires four companies (total to date = 8).

◆ 1996
Ships one millionth product.
Sales outside US surpass 50% of total revenue.
Acquires seven companies (total to date = 15).

◆ 1997
Appears first time in Fortune 500 – at #332.
Acquires six companies (total to date = 21).
Hires 10,000th employee.

◆ 1998
Acquires nine companies (total to date = 30).
Market capitalization reaches $100 billion – fastest company to that mark in history.

◆ 1999
Acquires 18 companies (total to date = 48).
Surpasses $10 billion annual revenue.

◆ 2000
Acquires six companies in first quarter
(total to date = 54).

to date. Having been with IBM and Wang when those companies rested on their laurels, he manages Cisco as if competitors will bury his firm tomorrow. Given today's competitive realities, someone could pull off such a feat. Given Cisco's ever-present concern for such an event, no one will.

NOTES

1. Friedman, Thomas L., "The Internet Wars," *New York Times*, 11 April 1998.

2. Schlender, Brent, "The Real Road Ahead," *Fortune*, 25 October 1999.

3. Hill, Andrew, "Shaping Up for the Net," *Financial Times*, 22 November 1999.

4. Compiled from numerous reports.

5. Friedman, Thomas L., "The Internet Wars," *New York Times*, 11 April 1998.

6. Roush, Matt, "Cisco Makes the Connection," *Business Marketing*, 1 August 1999.

7. Compiled from numerous reports.

8. Reinhardt, Andy, "The Man Who Hones Cisco's Cutting Edge," *Business Week*, 13 September 1999.

9. Ferguson, Charles H., *High Stakes, No Prisoners*, Times Business, New York, 1999.

10. Neff, Thomas J., and Citrin, James M., *Lessons from the Top: The Search for America's Best Business Leaders*, Currency-Doubleday, New York, 1999.

11. Cisco website: www.cisco.com, and Ries, Al, and Kinni, Theodore B., *Future Focus*, Capstone, Oxford, 2000.

One

MAKE YOUR PASSION YOUR BUSINESS – PREACH IT ALWAYS EVERYWHERE

IN THIS CHAPTER

As technological advances help erase the competitive advantages of product and service differentiations, it increasingly takes something more for a company to win and keep customers. It takes a deep-seated passion for your corporate mission, vision, and objectives – a bedrock belief that the world can't do without what you bring to it. This chapter reveals and discusses the elements of Cisco's passion, and how to make them yours, too.

From all outward appearances, Cisco Systems is a com pany filled with people who love their work and never tire of telling others why their company is tops in its field. Out front in this arena, as he should be, is Cisco President and CEO John Chambers. *Business Week* says, "His hawking is incessant. One day, he's preaching Net religion to Chinese President Jiang Zemin, and the next he's meeting with six geeks in a garage who are noodling over a new networking technology."[1]

As we enter the 21st century, forces of competition and demographics are compelling corporate executives to emulate the Cisco/Chambers model: pursue the career you love, and ensure that your people love what they're doing.

How so? Because you've got to love what you're doing to withstand the stresses of competition that is unprecedented in its scope and intensity. Because labor projections indicate that there will be 10 million more jobs than workers in the US by 2006.[2]

ABOVE ALL ELSE, DO WHAT YOU LOVE

John Chambers has a passion for his company and its business that seems to capture attention wherever he goes. Canada's *National Post*, commenting on one of Chambers' typically rousing speeches, noted that, "With his warm West Virginia drawl, a winning smile, and almost religious fervor about the content of his message, it is easy to imagine John Chambers in a pulpit."[3]

Others remark that Chambers' "fervor" is of an intensity usually restricted to that old-time religion. According to *The Arizona Republic*, Chambers "works the crowd of Fortune 1000 information officers a little like an evangelist – make that e-vangelist."[4] ABC-TV reporter Diane Sawyer called him "Chambers the evangelist, preaching the gospel of the Internet conversion." As if to confirm this assessment, Chambers told Sawyer, "I really am passionate about what I believe in."[5]

> "You can't keep [senior managers] here just by offering a paycheck. They don't need the money." – John Chambers

If she were to be apprised only of Cisco's phenomenal success, leadership consultant Janet E. Lapp would probably assert Chambers' passion even if she knew nothing about him. That's because Lapp believes "a sense of life-or-death urgency and great passion for the cause" are essential to leadership success. She notes, for example, that, "We saw urgency and passion in Colin Powell leading the military and Gandhi leading India to independence."[6]

As even a moment's thought about Powell's or Gandhi's mission makes clear, however, passion at the top is necessary but not sufficient for ultimate success. Passionate followers are also essential. So much so that James R. Lucas, in his book *The Passionate Organization*, asserts that, "The passionate organization will beat the big organization, the cash-rich organization, the savvy organization, and – yes – even the learning organization. The passionate organization . . . can alone bring the breakthroughs, the continuous improvement, the creativity, and the innovation to succeed big and demolish bored and boring foes."[7]

Cisco Systems, as a very practical matter, *must* employ people who are passionate about their work. Otherwise, as Chambers observes, they would be ineffective or lost to another organization.

> Because of our company's stock appreciation, almost everybody at the senior level is financially independent, so the only way to keep them is to keep them motivated, to have them want to work together as a team to accomplish something. You can't keep them here just by offering a paycheck. They don't need the money.[8]

TEN CLUES TO THE PRESENCE OF PASSION[9]

Is a passion of the sort shown by John Chambers and other Cisco employees present in the people you hire? Author James R. Lucas says you can find out by uncovering ten "clues to the presence of passion":

◆ *Willingness to confront reality.* A passion that builds value rather than destroying it always has to be based on reality.

◆ *Ability to discern the truth about who we are and what we want and need.* Is this person passionate about what is going on inside himself or herself?

◆ *Capacity to transform information and knowledge into wisdom* – by taking what we have learned and turning it into something useful and value-adding.

◆ *Alignment between personal and organizational aspirations.* Passionate people are interested in finding a kindred-spirit organization, not just a good job.

◆ *Desire to make a difference.* Ask, "How will we be different in five years if we hire, develop, and promote you?"

◆ *Love for labor.* Getting people motivated about work when they would rather be at the beach or fishing or whatever is hopeless.

◆ *Indignation over conditions.* Ask, "What makes you really mad?"

◆ *Evidence of battle scars.* If we've got passion, there are times when we just have to go to war.

◆ *An amateur's orientation.* Passion in a field of endeavor is kept alive by looking at the field from a constantly fresh perspective.

◆ *Being young at heart.* Thoreau said "No one is so old as he who has outlived his enthusiasm."

KNOW WHAT YOU'RE ABOUT AND KEEP IT ALWAYS IN SIGHT

Ask any Cisco employee about the company's objectives and he or she may "card" you – pull out a small card every employee carries that lists the firm's objectives (provided the person hasn't memorized them).

This is but one indicator of a fact of work-life among Cisco people: their work lives are suffused with the mission, vision, and goals that they have all bought into (literally, considering their generous and valuable stock options). "I am proud that we have a set vision in place," Chambers says. "We've determined the key elements by which we're going to measure our success and we are executing against them."[10]

In promulgating and promoting Cisco's objectives, Chambers again leads by example. Like all of the Cisco kids, his objectives card is with him always. And innumerable news articles mention Chambers' continual restatement of Cisco's principal objectives, as when *Business Week* recently noted that the company's desire to "change the way people live and work, play and learn . . . is an idealistic phrase that falls out of [Chambers'] mouth repeatedly and unabashedly."[11]

> "You don't sell the vision — someone either holds the core value or doesn't." — *Built to Last* coauthor Jerry I. Porras

That behavior would likely win praise from consultant Dennis G. McCarthy, who asserts that a company's mission must be communicated to employees "over and over again. And behavior of top executives must be consistent with the mission, or it becomes nothing more than hype."[12]

Making common currency of the corporation's reason for existing is essential, but only successful if stakeholders actually make progress toward their stated objectives. Cisco shines in this regard, also; the *National Post* noted that Chambers' enjoyment of "playing a role on the world stage . . . appears to stem less from being star-struck or self-important than it does from a feeling of delight that world leaders are actually getting it when he talks about the Internet revolution."[13]

THE GOSPEL ACCORDING TO JOHN

John Chambers' proselytizing on behalf of Cisco's vision and goals and impact of the Internet is likened by many observers to that of a preacher or revivalist on behalf of the deity and the great hereafter. Following is a selection of the "incessant" pronouncements he favors in meetings with employees, business executives, financial analysts, journalists, world leaders, and (presumably) the doormen of any hotel he enters:

◆ "The Internet revolution will bring together people with knowledge and information in virtual companies. And it will have every bit as much impact on society as the Industrial Revolution. . . . But instead of happening over 100 years . . . it will happen over seven years." [14]

◆ "The first industrial revolution combined people and factories and companies. The Internet revolution will combine people and information and will determine which will grow and survive and which will get left behind." [15]

◆ "I think this is the second Industrial Revolution. I don't think there is anything that could stop it. I think it is going to change the whole world, the way we work, live, play, and learn. [16]

◆ "If we do it right, we have the chance to become one of the most influential companies in history." [17]

◆ "If we execute properly, we are positioned to be the company that leads the Internet revolution." [18]

◆ "I think nice people can win. I don't think you have to be mean to be a good leader." [19]

◆ "I always listen to critics because often they're a good source of information for what you have to do differently. We take what we think they may be right [about] and make that a strength, not a limitation." [20]

> ◆ "We want to create unprecedented opportunities for our customers, our employees, our shareholders, and our partners."[21]
>
> ◆ "My greatest joy in life is communicating."[22]

CREATE AND KEEP A WINNING CULTURE

With characteristic understatement, John Chambers says, "Corporate culture is very important to us."[23] What can be learned from Cisco's approach to corporate culture that can be applied in other organizations? A review of expert analysis suggests the following guidelines.

Hire for cultural "fit"

While Cisco is known for its voracious appetite for other firms – 40 acquisitions in Chambers' first five years as CEO – the company claims to have rejected an even larger number of takeover targets at least partly due to cultural mismatch. That's in keeping with emerging thought and corporate performance, where employees' cultural "fit" with an organization is seen as more significant than ability or experience. For example, according to *The Washington Post,* superstar CEO Jack Welch of General Electric "is quite willing to toss out managers who don't sign on to the culture, even if they produce good results. 'We take people with great results and ask them to move on to other companies because they don't have our values.'"[24]

Among expert observers advocating a culture match, over and above a talents and responsibilities match, is Stanford Business

School's Jerry I. Porras, coauthor of *Built to Last*. He points to the critical importance of "alignment," resulting from activities such as determining "the five or six key behaviors we need in our people to realize our envisioned future. For example, everyone in the Disney organization must strive always to be pleasant to customers for customers to have the magical experience the company envisions."

This may be a trickier task than it seems, Porras notes, "because you don't sell the vision – someone either holds the core value or doesn't. The most that the leadership team can do is help people understand the vision." As for those who don't hold the core value, Porras contends that "you'll eventually have to part company, because, over the long haul, it's not good for the individual or the company to maintain the association. And in some cases this will be a very tough bullet to bite, because the person might in some ways – for example, technical expertise – be a valuable contributor to the organization."[25]

> **"What I really love about this place is the contest of ideas." – Cisco senior VP Howard Charney**

Cultural fit is also a big deal in the opinion of executive headhunter Millington F. McCoy, who says the nature of today's winning organizations – "less hierarchal, newly matrixed, and more global" – calls for managers who offer "not just a great resume, but a cultural fit with my client organization."[26]

Create an edgy, energetic workplace

In its earliest days, according to *Fortune* magazine,

> Cisco was the kind of mythical Silicon Valley startup that almost never happens anymore. [Founders] Bosack and Lerner mortgaged their house for seed capital. They borrowed against their credit cards. Lerner took a job with Schlumberger to support herself and her husband, while working for Cisco in every spare moment. Friends would gather in their living room to build routers and write code. [27]

The record of high-tech firms' ability to maintain the creative, frenetic atmosphere of their first years is mixed. IBM and Apple weren't able to keep the founding spirit alive, while Microsoft and Cisco most decidedly have.

Cisco gets bigger, but aims to act like "the biggest startup on the planet." – Cisco M&A chief Ammar Hanafi

Microsoft has clearly benefitted from the continuity afforded by the leadership of Bill Gates from Day One to the present. In *Hard Drive: Bill Gates and the Making of the Microsoft Empire*, authors James Wallace and Jim Erickson report,

> The corporate culture [has stayed] much the same: the work ethic, intensity, hard drive, creativity, youthfulness, and informality were woven into the very fabric of Microsoft from the start. People wore what they wanted to work, set their own hours, and had a variety of outside interests. But they were part of a team, a family. They shared a common goal and purpose, and it emanated first and foremost from Gates – work hard, make better products, and win. [28]

Another key to Microsoft's undiminished entrepreneurial energy is that Gates has consistently sought, indeed relished, employees who were unafraid of challenging any and all aspects of the firm's operations, from critical strategy, such as what to make of the Internet, to almost ludicrous detail, such as whether employees should be allowed in hallways with bare feet.

John Chambers' success in keeping Cisco creative and nimble is perhaps greater that Gates' – if only because Chambers entered the action comparatively late. Like Gates, though by somewhat different means, the Cisco CEO has kept his joint jumping. One key might be described as a remarkable inversion of the customary and expected course of culture melding following Cisco's acquisitions: Cisco, the acquirer, seems to soak up the high energy and entrepreneurial drive of its acquirees! The company gets bigger, but aims to act like "the biggest startup on the planet."[29]

Like Gates, Chambers also encourages challenge and dissent. Most famously, he holds monthly "birthday breakfasts," to which all employees with a birthday during the given month are welcomed and invited to raise any company-related question or issue with the CEO.

Admit no limits

Cisco's culture is one in which people are unconstrained by performance expectations based on what "should" be done or "could" be impossible. Never in history has a company so quickly achieved market capitalization of $100 billion. Never has a firm so consistently blown past analysts' consensus estimates of quarterly earnings growth. Never has a major US firm engaged in such a fast-paced, high-value acquisitions spree.

This record of records may be best explained by the company's bold – or, as some have said, "audacious" – statements of its role in the "new economy." Example: A Cisco regional sales director tells a prospective customer, "We are becoming synonymous with the Internet."[30] And why shouldn't he, when his superiors at the home office make similar statements? Chambers has claimed that Cisco is "the most influential company in history."[31]

Cisco is heeding in spirit, if not in fact, the advice of *Built to Last* authors Jerry Porras and James Collins to set "BHAGs – big, hairy, audacious goals." They say these bold stretch goals:

◆ should require 10 to 30 years to accomplish,

◆ must be concrete, easily and universally understandable, and

◆ above all, must be *not* easily achievable.[32]

Examples of BHAGs include the US space program's 1961 goal of putting man on the moon within the decade and Sony's 1950s goal of changing the worldwide poor-quality image of Japanese products. Long before the average working man could afford an automobile, Henry Ford stated a BHAG that said "everyone will have one."

In addition to formulating its BHAGs, Porras continues, company managers must articulate vivid descriptions of achieved goals. These describe conditions that will prevail when a BHAG is reached. Sony's triumph, for example, would mean that "our brand name is as well known as any in the world" and "made in Japan means something fine, not something shoddy." A candidate for a Cisco BHAG might be the expressed objective of leading the world into the new economy. What are your organization's BHAGs?

Never outgrow your culture

Incredibly, although Cisco is now a global outfit with a world-champion market capitalization, the company's "startup mentality" is reflected in "a corporate culture that is still ingrained at Cisco – and that still dazzles Wall Street."[33]

How has Cisco's culture fought off the afflictions of bureaucracy and smugness that seem to take hold when once-energetic firms grow large? One advantage is the company's positioning in what Chambers calls "the sweet spot – where technology and the future meet to transform not only business but all of life."[34] High energy comes easier for folks who go to work each day knowing their employer is playing a leading role in an industry that's changing the world.

As Selby Wellman, senior VP at Cisco's North Carolina installation, puts it, "Our goal is to shape the future of networking. That is an awesome responsibility. If that doesn't get you charged up in the morning, nothing will."[35] Another likely reason that greater size hasn't killed Cisco's golden-goose culture is the company's remarkable ability to retain employees gained through acquisitions. Howard Charney, who founded Cisco acquisition Grand Junction Networks and is now a Cisco senior VP, says, "What I really love about this place is the contest of ideas. Because we have people from different companies, there are different approaches to solving problems. That creates an atmosphere of excitement that even the best small company can't duplicate."[36]

FROM A CHILDHOOD LIMITATION, A VISION OF LIMITLESS GROWTH

Franklin D. Roosevelt overcame physical disability caused by polio to become the longest-serving US president. More recently, World War II hero Bob Dole rose to become US Senate majority leader and presidential candidate, despite grave and permanent battle injuries.

In these and other instances, might disability spur almost superhuman effort, leading to greater accomplishment than might have been achieved without a "handicap"?

We might ask such a question of Cisco CEO John Chambers. "I had what people now call a learning disability, probably what would be described as a mild form of dyslexia," he recounts. "And so, about second or third grade, I was having tremendous trouble in class."[37]

Chambers admits he felt dumb. Unable to keep up with classmates, he could sense the unvoiced "doubts" in the minds of teachers and parents. But he benefitted enough from a tutor hired by his parents to improve more than enough to stay in school and go on to earn college, law, and MBA degrees. Of the hurt he suffered from dyslexia, *Business Week* magazine says, "The experience fed his drive to succeed." It "pushed him to work harder than most."

The foremost lesson we can take from this, perhaps, is that Chambers – like FDR, Dole, and many others before him – didn't so much triumph over his disability as find a way to go around it and achieve nonetheless. Even today, he is reported to read as little as possible – never for pleasure – and compensate "with a remarkable memory."[38]

LEAD FROM A STATESMANLIKE STANCE

John Chambers and the company he heads win remarkably consistent favorable press coverage and expert commentary. That's no small achievement in an age when everyone from

Mike Wallace to Jay Leno is gleeful at the prospect of spit-roasting any Fortune 500 CEO, let alone the one who's made his firm the all-time speed-of-company-growth king.

What makes Chambers and Cisco media darlings? A big part of their appeal stems from appearing above the down-and-dirty competitive fray – advocating for their industry and lines of business far more than for their own products and services versus those of competitors. Chambers adopts "the role of industry statesman . . . to rise above the [competitive] acrimony," according to *Business Week*. "He has frequent meetings at the White House and hobnobs with Washington insiders during their pilgrimages to Silicon Valley. In the past year, he has met more than 30 heads of state."

"John Chambers is the single most competitive person I know." – UUNet chief John W. Sidgmore

It's important to note that we're talking here about the *appearance* of putting industry before company. WorldCom's UUNet chief John W. Sidgmore opines: "John Chambers is the single most competitive person I know."[39]

Of course it's considerably easier to avoid getting the dirt of competitive warring under one's fingernails when one holds an 80 percent market share in key product lines. Nonetheless, Chambers and other Cisco spokespersons appear comfortable extolling their industry rather than their brands, in much the same way as superstar athletes are quick to disclaim personal responsibility for their teams' victories, averring that "it was truly a team effort."

That analogy perhaps hints at why Coach Chambers and the

Cisco team can so magnanimously boost their industry: they have supreme confidence in their people, products, and services. So they're sure Cisco will win a sizable chunk of any new business their goodwill industry advocacy might create. Chambers has hinted as much: "Anything that helps the growth of the Internet helps Cisco, so we absolutely are the evangelists for the Internet."[40]

STAY ON MESSAGE IN EVERY FORUM

Cisco, like most major corporations, maintains a presence in a variety of public forums, ranging from television advertising to cause-related sponsorships. The strength of Cisco's communication in all media and events is its consistency and alignment with corporate vision and goals: we are the company that drives the Internet, the communications technology that is transforming the lives of everyone on earth.

Cisco's mass-media advertising is as lofty as Chambers' statesmanlike remarks on the "new world" economy. The networking giant's tag line – "Empowering the Internet generation" – is preceded by glimpses of the smiling faces of global-village citizens. Few of them – one might guess – would ever have even heard of Cisco Systems.

The ads take "an educational approach," as the trade publication *Advertising Age* called it, "with real people conveying facts such as: 'This month, another 18 million people will go online' and 'e-mail already outnumbers regular mail 10 to 1.'" Commenting on the underlying strategy, Cisco marketing head Keith Fox says, ''Everything we do is centered around the Internet."[41]

"Everything" includes Cisco's foremost ongoing charitable cause, the Cisco Networking Academy program, launched in September 1997, which provides instruction for high school and college students on how to design, build, and maintain computer networks. The company also sponsors the so-called Virtual Schoolhouse Grant program, which provides funds for US schools in remote areas or resource-poor districts to tap into the Internet. Cisco is a founding member of NetDay, another school wiring program, and – according to the corporate PR office – "was the first corporation to partner with the Internet2 program to define the next-generation Internet."

You may detect the hint of a theme here. It is different only in its delivery, not its content, from the single consistent message delivered "incessantly" by John Chambers. (And it of course leaves unspoken the fact that all of these schools, individuals, organizations, businesses, and governments that get online with the Internet create ever-greater demand in the 20 product and service lines in which Cisco holds the number 1 or 2 market-share position.)

Cisco's consistent message across all media and programs is in keeping with advice from Michael Lissack and Johan Roos in their book *The Next Common Sense: Mastering Corporate Complexity Through Coherence*. They argue that the most effective way for managers to cut through the increasing complexity they face today requires "the next common sense," which is demonstrated in coherence. "What coherence can do is enable actions to be grounded in certainty of purpose, identity, context, and further actions," they write.

Lissack and Roos illustrate by recounting the actions of Dee Hock as head of the then-infant credit card agency Visa. He faced the complexity of an organization made up of financial institutions that are fierce competitors – "constantly going after each other's customers" – but that had to cooperate in areas such as a common clearinghouse operation. When the Visa coalition was on the brink of collapse, with "no coherent viewpoint or actions," Hock got the organizing team to articulate a few key values around which the decentralized organization could cohere.[42]

Cisco's voice throughout the world is similarly coherent – and effective.

MAKE YOUR PASSION YOUR BUSINESS – PREACH IT ALWAYS EVERYWHERE

John Chambers is head cheerleader for a Cisco team that appears unified and dedicated to the overarching goal of networking the world – forging communication links that can overcome seemingly intractable problems of ignorance and poverty. These principles give their work its greatest meaning, and can do the same for you:

◆ **Above all else, do what you love.** Given the harsh realities of today's intense competition and continuous change, passion for your work is essential to achieve and sustain success.

◆ **Know what you're about and keep it always in sight.** The first step toward achieving anything is formulating a clear statement of what you want. A mission, vision, and goals are essential raw materials in any recipe for corporate success.

◆ **Create and keep a winning culture.** Your organization's culture is the bedrock required for building long-term success. It's not a set-and-forget proposition – your proactive attention keeps it alive and vibrant.

◆ **Lead from a statesmanlike stance.** When you provide the best-available products and services, you'll get more than your just share of sales just by selling people on your industry.

◆ **Stay on message in every forum.** Your customers are bombarded as never before by sellers extolling the merits of their offerings. To break through the din and win, you've got to reach people with a consistent, straightforward benefits statement.

NOTES

1. Reinhardt, Andy, "The Man Who Hones Cisco's Cutting Edge," *Business Week*, 13 September 1999.

2. Kaye, Beverly, and Jordan-Evans, Sharon, *Love 'Em or Lose 'Em: Getting Good People to Stay*, Berrett-Koehler, San Francisco, 1999.

3. Wheelwright, Geoffrey, "The World According to John Chambers: Cisco Vision," *National Post*, 20 September 1999.

4. Sidener, Jonathan, "Cisco Systems Executive Discusses Internet's Impact on World Economy," *Arizona Republic*, 24 September 1999.

5. ABC-TV, "20/20," 15 September 1999.

6. Author interview.

7. Lucas, James R., *The Passionate Organization*, Amacom, New York, 1999.

8. Neff, Thomas J., and Citrin, James M., *Lessons From the Top: The Search for America's Best Business Leaders*, Currency-Doubleday, New York, 1999.

9. Lucas, James R., *The Passionate Organization*, Amacom, New York, 1999.

10. Neff, Thomas J., and Citrin, James M., *Lessons From the Top: The Search for America's Best Business Leaders*, Currency-Doubleday, New York, 1999.

11. Byrne, John, "The Corporation of the Future," *Business Week*, 24 August 1998.

12. Author interview.

13. Wheelwright, Geoffrey, "The World According to John Chambers: Cisco Vision," *National Post*, 20 September 1999.

14. Friedman, Thomas L., "The Internet Wars," *New York Times*, 11 April 1998.

15. Wheelwright, Geoffrey, "The World According to John Chambers: Cisco Vision," *National Post*, 20 September 1999.

16. CNBC Network, "Street Signs," 10 June 1999.

17. Reinhardt, Andy, "The Man Who Hones Cisco's Cutting Edge," *Business Week*, 13 September 1999.

18. Thurm, Scott, "Cisco Net Rises 29%, Riding Web Growth," *Wall Street Journal*, 11 August 1999.

19. ABC-TV, "20/20," 15 September 1999.

20. Galarza, Pablo, "The Cisco Kid Takes on Telecoms," *Money*, July 1999.

21. Neff, Thomas J., and Citrin, James M., *Lessons from the Top: The Search for America's Best Business Leaders*, Currency-Doubleday, New York, 1999.

22. ABC-TV, "20/20," 15 September 1999.

23. Strassel, Kimberley A., and Hudson, Richard L., "European Firms Play Catch-Up on Web in Building Internet Technology," *Wall Street Journal*, 23 March 1999.

24. Swoboda, Frank, "Talking Management With Chairman Welch," *Washington Post*, 23 March 1997.

25. Author interview.

26. Author interview.

27. Nocera, Joseph, "Cooking with Cisco; What Does it Take to Keep a Hot Stock Sizzling?," *Fortune*, 25 December 1995.

28. Wallace, James, and Erickson, Jim, *Hard Drive: Bill Gates and the Making of the Microsoft Empire*, HarperBusiness, New York, 1992.

29. Donnelly, George, "Acquiring Minds," *CFO*, 1 September 1999.

30. Gomes, Lee, "The New Economy Is Still Being Driven by the Old Hard Sell," *Wall Street Journal*, 13 August 1999.

31. Laver, Ross, "Make Way for the Cisco Kid," *Maclean's*, 20 September 1999.

32. Author interview and Collins, James, and Porras, Jerry I., "Building Your Company's Vision," *Harvard Business Review*, September–October 1996.

33. Nocera, Joseph, "Cooking with Cisco; What Does it Take to Keep a Hot Stock Sizzling?," *Fortune*, 25 December 1995.

34. Byrne, John, "The Corporation of the Future," *Business Week*, 24 August 1998.

35. Keener, Adrianna, "Lucent Entry Charges Up Cisco's Chief," *[Raleigh, North Carolina] Triangle Business Journal*, 18 June 1999.

36. Plotkin, Hal, "Cisco's Secret: Entrepreneurs Sell Out, Stay Put," *Inc.*, March 1997.

37. ABC-TV, "20/20," 15 September 1999.

38. Reinhardt, Andy, "The Man Who Hones Cisco's Cutting Edge," *Business Week*, 13 September 1999.

39. Reinhardt, Andy, "The Man Who Hones Cisco's Cutting Edge," *Business Week*, 13 September 1999.

40. Cave, Andrew, "The Cisco Kid Grows Up to Be Mr. Internet," *Daily Telegraph*, 9 October 1999.

41. Elkin, Tobi, "Net Powerhouse Cisco Opens New Phase of Ad Effort," *Advertising Age*, 6 September 1999.

42. Lissack, Michael, and Roos, Johan, *The Next Common Sense: Mastering Corporate Complexity Through Coherence*, Nicholas Brealey, Naperville, Illinois, 1999.

Two

WIN THE WORLD WITH E-COMMERCE

IN THIS CHAPTER

Some observers view the rise of e-commerce as the most consequential transformation of world commerce since the rise of
mercantilism centuries ago. As a phenomenon of global and light-
speed proportions, it may be that – and more. The imperative for
companies is clear: take action at least as soon and as fast as any
competitor, or risk becoming a permanent also-ran. As a model for
action, you can do no better than to look at Cisco – and the measures described in this chapter that made the company the world's
leading e-commerce success story.

E-commerce – the online selling of everything imaginable (plus some things, such as human organs, that were once unimaginable) – is sweeping the globe. The growth rate of total e-commerce sales is on a trajectory so steep that some projections of "next year's" sales have been exceeded before the estimates were published. Best guesses as this volume was being prepared called for sales in 2003 totaling $1.3 trillion, up almost 3,000 percent in the five years since 1998, when online sales measured $43 billion.[1]

Cisco Systems has been out front and on top in Internet sales since the Net became a viable selling channel. But put aside (quickly!) any thought that only big companies or those in IT need be concerned with selling through the Net. In late 1999, *Business Week* remarked, "Now the Internet is cheap enough that even small job shops can afford to hook up. As a result, 'we'll see 90 percent of manufacturing move to the Internet' in short order, predicts [supply-chain research expert John J.] Fontanella."[2]

In a similar vein, London's *Financial Times* noted the considerable challenges confronting firms in the Internet economy. "But for many companies there may be no choice. As Stuart Brand, co-founder of Global Business Network, the consultancy and think-tank, said: 'When a new technology rolls over you, if you're not part of the steamroller, you're part of the road.'"[3]

A VERY BRIEF HISTORY OF E-COMMERCE'S VERY BRIEF HISTORY[4]

◆ **1996** – E-commerce begins with the arrival of static Web pages.

◆ **1997** – Websites gain dynamic, context-oriented capabilities.

◆ **1998** – Website content soars; advent of online auctions.

◆ **1999** – Retail and financial services enterprises personalize their e-commerce sales and customer service strategies. Early results indicate the effort is paying off like a rigged Las Vegas slot machine.

HOP ON THE E-COMMERCE "STEAMROLLER"

If you're at all intimidated by the task of getting your organization into e-commerce, take comfort in how it all began at Cisco Systems. There, in the mid-1990s, an employee named Chris Sinton was looking for new ways to sell Cisco-insignia products – the caps, pens, T-shirts, mugs, and other paraphernalia that mostly spread a company's name and perhaps make a few bucks as well. He assessed the possibilities of this new medium called the Internet – and the rest, as they say, is history. Literal, bona fide history: the report on the future of e-commerce that Sinton wrote for Cisco top management in 1995 is now preserved in the Smithsonian Institution archives. In 1998, Sinton, by then a member of top management himself, said, "I just knew the Net could be our business, that it could be a portal to our company."[5]

Oh, what a portal! According to *Business Week*, Cisco made one-third of all Internet sales in 1997, and in 1998 Cisco's Net sales were "nearly three times the Internet sales booked by pioneer Dell."[6] Today, Cisco gets about 80 percent of its orders over the Net – some $32 million worth every day.

The company's aggressive Net presence has boosted revenues per employee by 20 percent – to some $650,000 – versus an average $396,000 for the S&P 500 and $253,000 for top Cisco competitor Lucent Technologies.[7]

> In 1998 Cisco's Net sales were "nearly three times the Internet sales booked by pioneer Dell." – *Business Week*

Is your company capable of Cisco-like success with the Web? Such a question "raises thorny issues of strategy and organizational flexibility," according to *Harvard Management Update*. To answer it, the newsletter claims, you'll need to answer three key questions:

1. **Can you create a seamless customer experience?** You have to integrate your company across business units and products so that customers – who now have instant access to everything you sell – encounter no obstacles. Example: An insurance firm can't tell home buyers that mortgage insurance and homeowner's insurance are sold by different departments that require separate applications that ask for almost identical information.

2. **Can you deliver the goods?** "Companies offering their wares on the Web implicitly commit to doing business anywhere in the world, in any quantity . . . as fast and as cheaply as Web buyers expect." Your alternatives: Link to a partner skilled in logistics – for example, as Nike did with UPS – or go it alone – as, for instance, Amazon.com and eToys have.

3. **Can you get from here to there?** Don't laboriously formulate elaborate plans. Instead, "jump in, try out some strategies, and see what works. . . . Everybody's business models will continue to evolve."[8]

What's the imperative for your company to address these questions and grab a seat on the e-commerce "steamroller"? If jaw-dropping figures on increasing Internet sales don't convince you, consider this characterization of today's wired customers by a computer industry executive: "I don't want to fax you anymore, and I don't want to call you anymore. . . . We only want to do business with someone we can deal with electronically."[9]

"CISCO-SPEAK": LANGUAGE FOR THE INTERNET AGE

Here are brief explanations of a few of the Internet-related terms used most frequently by Cisco people:

◆ *Internet Ecosystem* – Cisco's annual report says it's "a new business model for Internet-connected businesses to serve Internet-connected customers." In much the same way as in a biological ecosystem, an Internet ecosystem comprises "a unique set of interwoven dependencies and relationships." Because Internet ecosystems are "open" – unlike, say, the famed electronic data links between Wal-Mart headquarters and all of its stores – "they encourage new members to participate and foster a collaborative relationship among members."

◆ *Internet years* – A term used by Chambers in much the same way as many of us use the term "dog years." According to Chambers, the Net and its attendant technologies speed the pace at which change occurs by a factor of about seven, such that the extent of change which previously occurred during a span of about seven years is now compressed into only one year. (One would presume this speeding up would be ideal for canines, whose year-length over their entire previous existence as a species has been one-seventh the length for humans, but few dogs are going digital.)

◆ *New World* – Applied as a descriptive adjective by Chambers and other Cisco kids to indicate anything Internet-related or otherwise "wired" – including the so-called "new economy" – that has or soon will overthrow anything and everything associated with the "old world." The latter, for Cisco, includes any ways of doing business before 1995 – particularly as still practiced by chief Cisco rivals Lucent and Nortel.

◆ *Second Industrial Revolution* – Chambers' often-mentioned synonym for "the Internet revolution," which he claims "will change everything . . . will transform every individual, every company, every country," but will play out in a few decades rather than the original Industrial Revolution's centuries-long run.[10]

BUILD YOUR OWN "INTERNET ECOSYSTEM"

Top Cisco officials – CEO Chambers in particular – love to talk about the "Internet ecosystem." That's not surprising, considering that (1) Chambers apparently invented the term, (2) Cisco surely has the most extensive, efficient, and (financially) healthy such ecosystem in the world, and (3) Cisco sells the vast majority of networking gear and services other organizations require to set up their own ecosystems.

An Internet ecosystem, in simplest terms, is a multi-party, multi-location electronic network. *Business Week* explains,

It seamlessly links Cisco to its customers, prospects, business partners, suppliers, and employees. . . . The network also is the glue for the internal workings of the company. It swiftly connects Cisco with its web of partners, making the constellation of suppliers, contract manufacturers, and assemblers look like one company – Cisco – to the outside world.[11]

There are profound implications for companies, countries, and even the global economy in the look, functioning, and pervasiveness of Internet ecosystems. If Chambers is wrong about their increasing importance – if the Internet in the long run settles into a role similar to that of the telephone – then Cisco Systems is likely at best to become the "Ma Bell" of the 21st century: an unspectacular but reliable utility.

But if Chambers is right – that Internet ecosystems are nothing less than the foundation of a "new world" economy – then:

◆ his company and countless "dot-com" start-ups will meet or exceed the spectacular future earnings the financial markets are attributing to them in current valuations;

◆ the durable, unstoppable, record-setting bull market and its attendant low-inflation, high-employment economy during the 1980s and 1990s will be merely prelude to good things in the 21st century; and

◆ *your* organization had better hook up its own Internet ecosystem.

All signs so far – even leaving aside what financial markets are saying by bidding money-losing dot-com IPOs to unprecedented valuations – are that Chambers is not merely right, but understating the implications of a world that's networking at a blinding pace.

Cisco is leading the way in leveraging its Internet ecosystem –
demonstrating what other organizations can do to fully exploit
the capabilities of e-business. What does this mean to you?
Business Week says,

> The network structure has vast implications for
> managing in the next century. GM's Sat-
> urn Division and Dell Computer
> have shown how the network
> can eliminate inventory, by
> connecting with partners that
> deliver goods only when they
> are needed. In the new model
> that Chambers is creating at
> Cisco, however, the network is perva-
> sive, central to nearly everything.[12]

> "The network
> structure has vast
> implications for managing
> in the next century." –
> *Business Week*

According to *The Washington Post*,

> This is what an electronic business looks like. Its supply chains
> and sales operations are all integrated electronically – provid-
> ing opportunities for instant flexibility and responsiveness. . . .
> Executive VP [Don] Listwin predicts that as American compa-
> nies become true electronic businesses, sharing information
> with customers and suppliers up and down the line, the produc-
> tivity impact 'is going to be 10 times what we're seeing today.'[13]

ENTER THE AGE OF CUSTOM-MADE EVERYTHING

Is your firm's ordering process the "dissatisfier"? That's the
term that was used by Linda Thom Rosiak to describe the
gauntlet to which Cisco customers were subjected back in
1995, when she was Cisco's new customer service chief. Dissat-
isfying was "the time and manpower it took to push orders
from Cisco's customers to its plants or suppliers," according to
Fortune. "The cause of the delays was the multitude of errors in

---

CISCO'S INCREDIBLE WEBSITE BY THE NUMBERS[14]

◆ Amount of data: 40 gigabytes

◆ Number of pages: 10 million

◆ Number of page views in a recent month: 40 million

◆ Number of software downloads from the site in a recent month: 380,000

◆ Number of order status checks in a recent month: 300,000

◆ Estimated customer service staff productivity improvement from online status checks alone: 15%

◆ Annual spending on new content and applications: $20 million to $30 million

◆ Number of content-development employees: 300–400

◆ Number of major site redesigns in five years: 6

◆ Frequency of small upgrades, improvements, and changes: daily

◆ Estimated total savings provided by the site in 1998: $600 million

---

the orders, which invariably arrived by fax." With hundreds of products and almost limitless combinations of options and features – not all of which work together – plus prices for 13,000 parts often pulled from out-of-date catalogs, Cisco received orders with the wrong prices or configurations 40 percent of the time. Recounts one customer: "We'd be faxing incorrect purchase orders back and forth. . . . Those errors could delay jobs for weeks."

More out of desperation that foresight, Rosiak put the sales process on the Internet. She and Cisco CIO Peter Solvik and their teams first came up with a program called Status Agent, which lets customers track the progress of their orders online. Next came posting the prices of all Cisco products. Third – and "most momentous of all" – was a program "that enabled customers to unerringly select compatible parts . . . for big-ticket items like routers." These are the principal components of Cisco Connection Online (CCO), which debuted in 1996 to wild acclaim of Cisco's customers. At Sprint, for example, "it used to take 60 days from the signing of a contract to complete a networking project. Now, thanks partly to the efficiency of ordering Cisco equipment online, it takes 35 to 45 days. Sprint has also been able to cut its order-processing staff from 21 to six, allowing the other 15 employees to work instead on installing networks." A Sprint official says, "We are doing more and more projects where Cisco is supplying all the equipment. It's just faster that way."[15]

> A Sprint official says, "We are doing more and more projects where Cisco is supplying all the equipment. It's just faster that way."

And that, in a nutshell, is the secret to gaining *greater* profitability through what's known as "mass customization" – building every item to a customer's exact specifications – as practiced most famously by Dell Computer. "With Internet commerce, you're dealing in lots of 'eaches,' not a truckload of identical products," says Denver software executive Michael A. Schmitt. Each order represents a unique mix of parts that can trigger dozens or even hundreds of purchase orders to suppliers. "If you tried to handle all this on paper and over the phone, it would never get done," Schmitt adds. "Computers have to talk to other computers."[16]

The potential for leveraging emerging technologies to customize entire product lines was seen early by consultant Don Peppers, coauthor of *Enterprise One to One: Tools for Competing in the Interactive Age.* "A one-to-one enterprise treats different customers differently . . . customizing products to [their] specifications," he explains. That sounds costly, "But we believe that one-to-one marketing, done right, is cost-effective over time," Peppers adds. "Take the classic example: Levi's 10,000 size combinations in women's jeans. They custom-produce jeans for every customer – whose measurements are taken in the store and sent electronically for production. Among other savings, there's no inventory risk for the company."

More important: "Every time I as a supplier interact with you as a customer, I get a little tighter to meeting your complete and precise preferences," Peppers says. "And I'm making it more and more difficult for you to have any interest in my competitors."[17]

TIPS FROM CISCO FOR A SUPERSTAR WEBSITE[18]

◆ Centralize: design, organization, and information architecture (in corporate marketing).

◆ Decentralize: content (to each business unit – "each function best understands what the customer needs").

◆ Open information to customers – status of the order, pricing, options, etc. Reason: Eliminate customer calls to sales reps.

◆ Market the site in media tightly focused on your target customers. "If you build it, they will not necessarily come."

◆ Market the site to employees – make sure they know what's there and how customers use the site.

◆ Continually gauge effectiveness, ease-of-use, and desired enhancements – through customer surveys, focus groups, advisory panels, and informal contacts.

SUPPLY-CHAIN MAGIC: STOP MAKING ANYTHING – BUT MONEY

Aside from making profits to the tune of about a 30 percent margin, Cisco Systems doesn't make much of anything. That's no insult, it's what John Chambers dubs "virtual manufacturing." He explains it as "the ability to run your global plants as though they were one. . . . We deal with 34 plants globally, and 32 aren't owned by us."[19]

Executive VP Don Listwin had a slightly different term for the same philosophy: "You've heard of just-in-time manufacturing. Well, this is not-at-all manufacturing."[20]

Business Week quantifies the process:

> "You've heard of just-in-time manufacturing. Well, this is not-at-all manufacturing." – Cisco Executive VP Don Listwin

[Cisco] suppliers not only make all the components and perform 90 percent of the subassembly work but even do 55 percent of the final assembly. So suppliers regularly ship finished Cisco computers to Cisco customers without a Cisco employee ever touching the gear. The result is "savings of between $500 million and $800 million" in 1999, compared to what it would cost to own and operate those plants, says Carl Redfield, Cisco's senior vice president for manufacturing.

Redfield proceeds to describe how Cisco avoids the out-sourcing risk of losing the manufacturing expertise that contributes to continuing product improvements. "We develop the entire [production] process, and we know what every supplier is doing every moment. The source code for all this is developed here and maintained here. So the innovation is all here."

Virtual manufacturing isn't only a Cisco thing. "Hewlett-Packard, IBM, Silicon Graphics, and others have sold plants to contract producers such as Solectron, SCI Systems, Flextronics, and Celestica – then signed up these manufacturing specialists as suppliers," *Business Week* reports. "Some experts imagine that many enterprises will ultimately become tripartite virtual partnerships. One arm will handle product development and engineering, another will take care of marketing, and the third will do the production chores."[21]

One expert who would affirm that possible course is Jim Emshoff, who heads outsourcing consultants IndeCap Enterprises Inc. He previously headed MedQuist Inc., a company that entered what Emshoff calls "a then-stagnant medical transcription industry." By meeting "the then-unmet needs of its customers – hospitals – MedQuist created the interactive electronic medical record business, which today is growing about 20 percent annually."

Such innovation, Emshoff contends, "is perhaps the greatest single benefit of outsourcing." That and other benefits more than compensate, he claims, for what sometimes appears on paper as a higher cost for outsourcing than traditional do-it-yourself. "It may be more only in terms of the company's outlay, but clearly [outsourcing] will even more often add value that outweighs the additional cost."

He provides an example by again citing MedQuist:

> The turnaround time on medical transcription of physicians' notes historically averaged from two days to a week – well after the notes could aid immediate decision making. But with technological advances of outsource providers – in this case, MedQuist's development of the electronic medical record – transcribed notes can be available to caregivers in hours, even minutes, as a patient moves through treatment.

Emshoff challenges notions that outsourcing adversely affects employee loyalty.

> When outsourcing is done right, loyalty of the supplier's employees is enhanced, because the workers have more opportunities to advance. That's what a medical transcriber gets with a company that only does medical transcription, or what a mail clerk gets when the employer only runs mail rooms.[22]

London's *Financial Times* recently noted that not every firm will emerge a winner from the wave of outsourcing. Supply-chain "intermediaries," the paper noted, citing a report from consultants Booz-Allen & Hamilton, "have a new imperative: add value or risk being cut out entirely. . . . At the same time the Internet makes it easier for companies to focus on what they do best – their core activity – and spin off or contract out other operations to their 'wired' partners."[23]

SERVICE-CHAIN MAGIC: SAVE THE COST OF 1,000 ENGINEERS

In 1994, Cisco's Technical Assistance Center was facing a staffing crisis. As recounted by *Fortune* magazine, "highly trained

SOME OUTSOURCING CONSIDERATIONS[24]

Outsourcing to the extent Cisco practices can be advantageous, but it's not a no-brainer. Here are some criteria for evaluating whether to outsource an activity:

◆ *Know why you're looking at outsourcing*. Don't copy your competitors or jump on a bandwagon. Look closely at your own situation. Outsourcing is *not* a strategy; it's a possibly better way to *pursue* a strategy.

◆ *Consider whether other measures should come first*. You may benefit more from a technique such as process reengineering than from outsourcing.

◆ *Conduct an open investigation*. Let any potentially affected employees know what you're doing and why. Reasons: They'll find out through the grapevine if not from management, and they'll be able to give your outside consultants and bidders a complete picture of the work to be done.

◆ *Determine whether the activity is a core competency*. If it is – as Website management is for Cisco – favor retaining the activity. If it's not, add points to the outsource side.

◆ *Weigh possible gains from innovation*. Consultant Jim Emshoff says innovation is perhaps the greatest single benefit of outsourcing. "Entire new industries are being created on the strength of outsource providers' innovative practices."

◆ *Think value, not cost*. Outsourcing will seldom look better based on cash outlay alone. But other factors – staff vacancies, expertise, and other intangibles – may more than compensate.

and extremely scarce" service engineers were spending most of their days "fielding routine questions about minor malfunctions" of Cisco networking gear, "leaving not enough time to deal with the really tough technical challenges." TAC chief Brad Wright's solution: "Automate all the routine stuff on the Internet and let buyers serve themselves."

Within three months, "Wright's team had put the most frequent questions on the Web. It also set up a program that let customers choose and download software. The reaction was astounding. Weary of playing phone tag with busy engineers from nine to five, customers flocked to the Internet for effective 24-hour service. Calls and faxes dwindled." Result: Over the next three years, while sales jumped fourfold, Cisco's engineering support staff only doubled, to 800. "Without automated sales support, Cisco estimates it would need well over 1,000 additional engineers." Estimated savings: $325 million a year, not including "the billions in sales the company might have forgone if it hadn't been able to find those 1,000 extra engineers."[27]

> "Without automated sales support, Cisco estimates it would need well over 1,000 additional engineers."
> — *Fortune*

Today, according to *Internet Week*,

> Cisco is providing about 80 percent of its customer service over the Internet. [Cisco CIO Peter] Solvik says customer connections are provided through a private extranet to ensure security. The company is also working to offer more direct connections for its customers, although nothing is ready to be tested. "We're moving toward linking customer networks

directly to ours to work with customers proactively," Solvik says.[26]

EXTEND THE PERSONAL TOUCH WITH "IMPERSONAL" E-WARE

At first, it seems impossible: By *lessening* person-to-person interaction – interposing the supposedly impersonal electronics of the Internet – you can *increase* the customer's perceived individual attention. If you still think it's impossible, you've never been a customer of Cisco Systems, or Amazon.com. These e-commerce customer-service trailblazers, plus others, have brilliantly employed the power of automation to make customers feel special.

> **"[Cisco's] Listwin shows me that day's top 10 customers, then focuses down to what the company sold that day in Asia – specifically in China, specifically to telephone companies. It's all there." – Washington Post**

Consider, for example, this snapshot of Cisco executive VP Don Listwin, as related in *The Washington Post*: "Listwin shows me that day's top 10 customers, then focuses down to what the company sold that day in Asia – specifically in China, specifically to telephone companies. It's all there. 'Let's see where we're having problems,' says Listwin. He moves to a screen called 'Critical Accounts.' Any customer can put itself on this watch list and get instant, daily attention from top management."[27]

Internet Week reports that IBM officials estimate their 1999 service transactions conducted via the Internet – with no human intervention – numbered some 28 million. A company official said these customers are "some of our most satisfied. They're getting answers when they need them." Anticipated savings: $600 million.[28]

How are such savings consistent with greater customer satisfaction? Richard G. Barlow, who heads Frequency Marketing, Inc., notes that automated interaction exploits computer and communications technology, but cautions against thinking that what's happening is really new. "It all comes down to individual relationships with customers, which is precisely where the mom-and-pop retailers of yesterday excelled. I grew up in a crowded urban neighborhood, where the owners of the corner store drew 99 percent of their customers from within a two-block radius. They knew their customers so well that they would order extra apples for Aunt Martha's pies when that lady made her annual visit to the McCauley's up the street."

For similarly successful customer relationships today, Barlow contends, "You must accept the challenge of segmenting the customer base. . . . The technology exists; what's needed is the commitment."[29]

According to e-marketing guru Don Peppers, British Airways has demonstrated such commitment. Computer software developed by the airline allows the company to track and respond to the flying preferences of individual passengers. "So when I fly, the flight attendant doesn't ask what I want to drink. Instead, he or she says, 'Here's your caffeine-free Diet Pepsi, Mr. Peppers.'" There's incredible power in that simple statement, according to Peppers. "On a previous flight, they learned what I prefer to drink. On this flight, they may learn that London is usually a connecting stop for me, not my destination. On future flights, they'll keep adding to what they know about me."

That describes what Peppers calls a "learning relationship" with customers, a relationship "that makes it almost impossible for a customer to leave you." The reason: "The customer knows that he or she would have to start all over with any other provider – even if that provider was just as good as you in forming learning relationships. Unless you do something the customer thinks is really, really awful, he or she won't want to leave – and won't be able to leave – without significant personal inconvenience."

And such a relationship with customers may involve little or no cost. Peppers says that British Airways originally developed its customer-tracking software as a cost-reduction measure. "They don't have to load so much food and drink on a flight if they know what passengers will want." But, "at the cost of a few pennies for my soft drink, they go a long way toward ensuring I'll keep choosing to fly with them."[30]

"IQ" TEST OF YOUR COMPANY'S INTERNET READINESS[31]

Cisco's Internet Quotient (IQ) self-assessment test is a qualitative measure for determining a company's potential in the Internet economy. By answering the following series of 20 questions, Cisco says, you can determine your company's own IQ.

Category 1: Operations Ecosystem

1. Management Vision: Is senior management actively engaged and driving an Internet strategy throughout all areas of your company? Yes/No

2. Business/IT Partnership: Are your company's business and Internet strategies well integrated? Yes/No

3. Customer Connectedness: Are your company's Internet applications driven by customer needs? Yes/No

4. E-Learning: Is your company promoting knowledge transfer about its Internet Activities? Yes/No

5. Adaptive Technology Infrastructure: Are your company's Internet solutions flexible to accommodate rapid change and scalability? Yes/No

6. E-Commerce: Are your company's Internet activities - Internet sales, marketing, support, operations - a critical component of the company's success? Yes/No

7. Ecosystem Potential: Does your company have a track record in building and managing multiple strategic relationships with complementary players? Yes/No

8. Employee Empowerment: Are employees encouraged to initiate Internet activities that create new customer value and greater productivity? Yes/No

9. Executing in Internet Time: Does your company exhibit "Ruthless Execution" (3 months or less) in the deployment of its Internet strategy? Yes/No

10. Internet Returns: Does your company have an established metrics that prioritizes and drives Internet activities? Yes/No

Category 2: Market Ecosystem

11. Partnership: Is your company a preferred business partner? Yes/No

12. Market Vision: Does your company have a view of the future that is attractive to other companies? Yes/No

13. Internet Standards: Does your company actively participate in Internet standards development for your industry? Yes/No

14. Community Building: Does your company create communities where customers interact with other customers? Yes/No

15. Developer Community: Is your company creating opportunities for other companies to profit from its business? Yes/No

16. Global Presence: Does your company's Internet strategy eliminate geographical boundaries? Yes/No

17. Market Innovation: Are third parties spontaneously adding value to or innovating around your company's Internet strategy? Yes/No

18. Market Position: Do third parties support the marketing of your company's Internet story to customers? Yes/No

19. Venture Capital Endorsed: Are venture capitalists funding innovations that are consistent with your company's Internet strategy? Yes/No

20. Strategic Investment: Is your company investing in its future by funding companies or entrepreneurs that complement its Internet strategy? Yes/No

Scoring

In the Operations Ecosystem category (Questions 1–10), give your company one point for every "Yes" answer. In the Market Ecosystem category (Questions 11–20), give your company two points for every "Yes" answer. Separately add your total points for each of the two categories. The final score is calculated by multiplying the sum of the Operations category by the sum of the Market category. *Example:* 7 "Yes" answers in the Operations Ecosystem category and 6 "Yes" answers in the Market Ecosystem category would result in a score of 84: $(7 \times 1) \times (6 \times 2) = 84$.

Your Company's Internet Quotient (IQ): _____

Interpretation

160–200 = Internet Visionary: Aggressively experiment with a community of interest in your industry as well as complementary upstream/downstream players.

120–160 = Internet Expert: Promote Internet successes to the investment community, customers, employees, and suppliers.

80–120 = Internet Savvy: Gain momentum through quick Internet projects with 3–6 month delivery cycles.

40–80 = Internet Aware: Create a SWAT team that will create an immediate sense of urgency throughout the organization. Within 1–3 months this team should report back to the CEO and Board on Internet opportunities.

0–40 = Internet Agnostic: Educate senior management by sending them to visit Internet leaders and engaging them with industry best practices.

WIN THE WORLD WITH E-COMMERCE

E-commerce can be much more than a way to make sales. Done right, it can provide the means for a company to establish a web of connectivity that efficiently links it to customers, suppliers, and partners in win-win relationships that can lead to unprecedented profitability. Cisco has pioneered such arrangements; you can reap their benefits:

◆ **Hop on the e-commerce "steamroller."** You don't have to set out to conquer the world to get into e-commerce. Cisco was at first seeking only a new way to sell its promotional insignia products. But your organization, like Cisco, must seize on great ideas from any corner of the organization and make the most of an initially limited e-commerce adventure.

◆ **Build your own "Internet ecosystem."** If there ever was an era of stubborn independence in world commerce, it's decidedly gone forever. You've got to forge links to form a network that provides unprecedented flexibility and responsiveness.

◆ **Enter the age of custom-made everything.** Today's technologies – led by the Internet – don't merely allow custom orders, but make them the most efficient way to fill orders. In many industries, such "mass customization" is becoming essential for corporate survival.

◆ **Supply-chain magic: stop making anything – but money.** In an increasingly interconnected world, the only way to meet customers' ever-changing needs is to stick to your company's core competencies and go to partners and suppliers for everything else.

◆ **Service-chain magic: save the cost of 1,000 engineers.** No company can grow its profitability if costs increase in lockstep with revenue. The Internet provides the most powerful tool ever for passing the benefits of an expanding customer base to the bottom line.

◆ **Extend the personal touch with "impersonal" e-ware.** The best customer care can result from *less* person-to-person customer contact. You can use the most modern technologies to deliver the best of old-fashioned individual attention.

NOTES

1. Belton, Beth, "Net's Economic Impact Zooms," *USA Today*, 10 June 1999.

2. Byrne, John, "The Search for the Young and Gifted," *Business Week*, 4 October 1999.

3. Taylor, Paul, "Online Revolution Set to Overthrow Many Established Practices, *Financial Times*, 19 July 1999.

4. Coleman, David, and Ward, Lewis, "Hands-On E-Business: Improve customer experiences and increase sales with collaborative commerce," *E-Business Advisor*, September 1999.

5. Tully, Shawn, "How Cisco Mastered the Net," *Fortune*, 17 August 1998.

6. Byrne, John, "The Corporation of the Future," *Business Week*, 24 August 1998.

7. Reinhardt, Andy, "The Man Who Hones Cisco's Cutting Edge, *Business Week*, 13 September 1999.

8. Uncredited, "Is Your Company Capable of Competing on the Web?," *Harvard Management Update*, June 1999.

9. Gillooly, Caryn, "Tech Companies Want Everything On The Web," *InternetWeek*, 27 September 1999.

10. Van, Jon, "Cisco Chief: Prepare For Internet Changes," *Chicago Tribune*, 1 October 1999.

11. Byrne, John, "The Corporation of the Future," *Business Week*, 24 August 1998.

12. Byrne, John, "The Corporation of the Future," *Business Week*, 24 August 1998.

13. Ignatius, David, "Online in the New Economy," *Washington Post*, 11 July 1999.

14. Roush, Matt, "Cisco Makes the Connection," *Business Marketing*, August 1999.

15. Tully, Shawn, "How Cisco Mastered the Net," *Fortune*, 17 August 1998.

16. Port, Otis, "Customers Move into the Driver's Seat," *Business Week*, 4 October 1999.

17. Author interview.

18. Roush, Matt, "Cisco Makes the Connection," *Business Marketing*, August 1999.

19. Jones, Del, and Belton, Beth, "Cisco Chief: Virtual Close to Hit Big," *USA Today*, 12 October 1999.

20. Port, Otis, "Customers Move Into the Driver's Seat," *Business Week*, 4 October 1999.

21. Port, Otis, "Customers Move Into the Driver's Seat," *Business Week*, 4 October 1999.

22. Author interview.

23. Taylor, Paul, "Online Revolution Set to Overthrow Many Established Practices, *Financial Times*, 19 July 1999.

24. Stauffer, David, "Are Corporate Staffs on the Way Out?," *Across the Board*, May 1998.

25. Tully, Shawn, "How Cisco Mastered the Net," *Fortune*, August 1998.

26. Gillooly, Caryn, "Tech Companies Want Everything On The Web," *InternetWeek*, 27 September 1999.

27. Ignatius, David, "Online in the New Economy," *Washington Post*, 11 July 1999.

28. Gillooly, Caryn, "Tech Companies Want Everything On The Web," *InternetWeek*, 27 September 1999.

29. Author interview.

30. Author interview.

31. Cisco corporate website: www.cisco.com.

Three

USE THE NET TO REVOLUTIONIZE INTERNAL OPERATIONS

IN THIS CHAPTER

Advantages of the Internet don't only extend outward from the company's doors. Cisco's administrative and support units are extensively using the Internet and its corporate intranet for a startling range of programs and activities. This chapter suggests ways that almost any organization can gain from getting wired in functions where media reports consistently cite Cisco for best practices.

Cisco doesn't stop leveraging the incredible power of electronic interconnections with its Internet ecosystem, described in the previous chapter. The company is also among world leaders in applying Net advantages to internal and administrative activities.

For a glimpse of the efficiencies that can flow from inside wiring, consider a *Washington Post* reporter's account of a visit with Cisco executive VP Donald Listwin: "He goes to a screen that records capital spending proposals. A request to buy $188,000 worth of Sun computers is awaiting his approval. He types a few keystrokes and – bing! – the order is made. The entire process took about 10 seconds."[1]

CISCO'S INTERNAL NET NUMBERS[2]

◆ Current lag between quarterly close of business and close of books: 24 hours

◆ Target lag between quarterly close of business and close of books: 1 hour

◆ Intranet hits per month from employees: 11 million

◆ Share of job applications received by Internet: 81%

◆ Share of new hires whose first contact was by Internet: 66%

◆ Number of days by which Cisco has reduced average job vacancy period by using the Internet: 68

◆ Cisco's recruiting cost per hire: $6,556. Industry cost: $10,800

TURN INFORMATION SYSTEMS INTO A COMPETITIVE ADVANTAGE

The chances are good that your company views information systems (IS) in much the same way as payroll, finance, and other staff units: lots of required spending with no offsetting revenues. That's the traditional and still prevailing view.

But that's not the way Cisco sees IS. According to John Chambers,

"[In one] year we saved $500 million on an expense base of $2 billion through seven Web-based applications."

We began to shift the information systems function from an expense item, which it was when I got here, into a competitive advantage. [In one] year we saved $500 million on an expense base of $2 billion through seven Web-based applications. We put that back into R&D and distribution. We save more each year than our nearest competitor spends on R&D. You don't have to explain to a nontechnology businessperson what that means in terms of competitive advantage.[3]

It's unlikely that any single use of IS for competitive advantage holds more promise than what Chambers calls the "virtual close." Imagine closing your company's books and having detailed financial reports at employees' fingertips within in hour of the close of any reporting period – week, month, or quarter. That's Cisco's "virtual close" target – which they expect to achieve in 2000.

Chambers recognizes the benefits when employees are empowered with an almost instant numerical picture of operations. "We know exactly what is occurring in individual product lines, in our supply chain, and in our inventory."[4]

The potential benefits? Chambers cites these:

The ability to close so quickly lets you spot problems and opportunities at any time. It allows you to see what's going on in every aspect of your business. . . . Normally, executives might not see things until after the quarter has ended. . . . Virtual close lets you be proactive, rather than reactive. You can know what your expenses are in a given geography or exactly what your margins are by product line. . . . Suppose sales jump 30 percent in Latin America overnight. With the virtual close, a team could be sent down there immediately to analyze and exploit it.[5]

"Suppose sales jump 30 percent in Latin America overnight. With the virtual close, a team could be sent down there immediately to analyze and exploit it."

Chambers' words indicate that he appreciates the importance of emphasizing the 'I' in IS, as advocated by renowned management guru Peter F. Drucker in *Management Challenges for the 21st Century*. He observes that managers who use information can't expect their IS or MIS departments or CIOs to appropriately emphasize the 'I,' because "the producers of data cannot possibly know what data the users need so that they become information. And only individual knowledge workers, and especially individual executives, can decide how to organize their information so that it becomes their key to effective action."

The "ultimate test" of whether data is being provided as useful and meaningful information, Drucker writes, "is that there are no surprises. Before events become significant, executives have already adjusted to them, analyzed them, understood them, and taken appropriate action." To achieve this goal, executives must be able "to eliminate data that do not pertain and to organize the data, to analyze, to interpret – and then to focus the resulting information on action. For the purpose of information is not knowledge. It is being able to take the right action."[6]

HIRE BETTER–FASTER–CHEAPER WITH THE WEB

When you're in the job market – either looking for work or looking to hire – the Internet is increasingly the place to meet your match. The Net appears to be "the new face of job hunting," according to *Fortune* magazine, an assertion backed by Intel Chairman Andy Grove, who says, "Digital resumes, digital employment advertising, digital resume searches – it's a rebuilding of the infrastructure. It's almost following e-mail in its growth."[7]

And the biggest user in the big trend toward Net-based recruiting is Cisco Systems. In a job market that's extremely tight in general and suffocatingly tight in finding the kind of brainy, creative software-engineer types Cisco often needs, the company's website is "a venus flytrap of attractions," according to *Fortune*: "Visitors can fill a shopping cart with job openings that interest them or join the Make Friends @ Cisco program, which connects them with a real-life person from the department in which they want to work."

Payoffs for Cisco from going so heavily to the Net for recruiting abound, led by the statistical improvement considered most important by HR chief Barbara Beck: an average period it takes to fill a job that's down to 45 days in 1999 from 113 days three years earlier. Also impressive is Cisco's savings: Its average recruiting cost per new hire is more than $4,000 less than for the IT industry as a whole. And the company's recruiting staff has held steady at about 100 while its annual rate of hiring has soared from 2,000 to 8,000 people.[8]

Although Cisco still accepts mailed resumes with traditional cover letters, their spokespersons strongly hint that the candidate who goes that route rather than using the Net is battling a two-strike count before the envelope is opened. A Cisco HR team leader at the company's Research Triangle, North Carolina, location, for example, notes that it takes longer for paper resumes to be scanned into electronic databases and routed to the right person. "The hiring process has really sped up," that recruiter observes.[9]

> Because Cisco recruits largely through the Internet, its recruiting cost per new hire is more than $4,000 less than for the IT industry as a whole.

Lest you think the preference for hiring online is nothing more than a fleeting fad, consider that Cisco's next significant resume scanning enhancement, according to *Business Week*, is "textually analyzing the resumes of successful hires, then using that knowledge to screen incoming resumes more efficiently."[10] Heed also the words of Hewlett-Packard staffing manager Bruce Hatz, who says a Net search for good people is "dramatically more effective than any medium ever known. The Web is the future of recruiting."[11]

HOP ABOARD THE E-TRAIN

It is probably an exaggeration to say that employee training and the Internet's capabilities pair up as a marriage made in heaven. But not too much of one.

TIPS FOR POSTING A WINNING WEB RESUME[12]

◆ De-emphasize verbs (e.g. "I *drove* the inventory initiative); favor nouns (because human and automated scanners are looking for keywords, e.g. *software, technology, project*).

◆ Organize by KSA – knowledge, skills, abilities – rather than by chronology.

◆ Don't use typeface enhancements, such as italics and boldface. Databases get confused by the computer coding and scanning machines can misread typeface changes – as when one applicant's "cum laude" was reproduced as "corn dude."

◆ Say "cheese." Job boards will increasingly promote capability to attach short video clips to online resumes.

Because the most attractive features of the Internet – such as instant worldwide access and ease of updating material – directly address some of the most nettlesome bugaboos of company training – such as ever-climbing travel costs, inconsistency of content from trainer to trainer and location to location, and becoming instantly outdated in the face of any changes in products, procedures, or technologies.

John Chambers refers to this same beautiful relationship when he says, "There are two fundamental equalizers in life: the Internet and education." E-learning combines these equalizers, he says, to revolutionize the way organizations around the world communicate and train their people. Such sentiments indicate why Cisco announced in November 1999 that it would shift all corporate training to what the company calls "an e-learning model," applicable to all corporate training offered to employees, partners, and customers.[13]

Cisco CIO Peter Solvik says the company's training focus currently "is on our own employees." They typically initiate "just-in-time learning" by making a request over the company intranet. In some cases, a pre-test is delivered to the employee; it helps determine whether the specific course requested is appropriate for the employee and his or her immediate needs. Next, "the corresponding training module for that course would be transmitted overnight – when network traffic would be least affected," relates the publication *Internet Week*. "Completing the cycle, information on which employees take and complete specific courses is automatically fed into the human resources database. This allows Cisco to keep track of which employees have particular skills." The entire "closed-loop system" helps reduce travel costs for the company and, more important in a tight labor market, improves employee retention.[14]

PLUSES CISCO SEES IN NET-BASED TRAINING[15]

◆ Inexpensively delivers instructional content in multiple formats.

◆ Provides flexibility and convenience of reaching students anywhere, any time. They're free to study at their own pace, regardless of location.

◆ Allows learners to obtain relevant information faster, increase their own productivity, and move forward or repeat course sections based on performance.

◆ Permits easy management and tracking of learning by students' instructors and managers.

◆ Provides company-wide access to an extended network of learners, instructors and experts.

◆ Allows quick and easy reuse and reformatting of content, significantly reducing development and delivery time.

◆ Permits online testing with instant results and feedback.

BECOME AN E-LEARNING ORGANIZATION

"The new economy is heavy on intellectual capital," John Chambers says. "The sharing of knowledge is what really makes it go."[16]

With these words, Chambers acknowledges the increasing primacy of the knowledge worker in today's global economy and correctly implies that sustained corporate success in the 21st century will be possible for companies that find effective ways to share knowledge organization-wide. Today, as journalist Thomas A. Stewart, author of *Intellectual Capital: The New Wealth of Organizations*, notes, "even a heavy industry such as petroleum sees more than 50 percent of the cost of extracting oil spent on knowledge." That marks a transformation that's been effectively addressed by few companies, Stewart observes. The typical manufacturer knows the exact cost of every raw material in its products, but has not identified the who, when, and how much of intellectual inputs. That's important, Stewart contends, "because, as a manager, your job is to find ways to turn individualized knowledge into shared knowledge. Companies that don't do this spend all kinds of time reinventing the wheel. They also lose the knowledge of any worker who leaves, when they would have kept it if it had been shared."[17]

Today's electronic networking – made possible by the very products and programs Cisco produces – makes instant, global, organization-wide knowledge sharing possible. But John Chambers clearly recognizes that the network only makes knowledge sharing *possible*. To make it *happen*, executives must make real the employee empowerment that in many organizations is the subject of too much talk and little or no action.

That imperative was recognized early in the knowledge-sharing transformation of Buckman Laboratories – an effort that might serve as a model for other organizations. Company founder Robert H. Buckman relates that he and his colleagues concluded that "we had to empower every one of our associates to contact directly any other associate, at any level or location of the organization."

That conclusion was "inescapable," Buckman says, based on findings about his firm that aren't far different from thousands of others:

◆ The company's 1,300 employees are scattered in some 90 countries and collectively speak 15-plus native languages.

◆ With the combination of time zones and travel and other factors, 86 percent of all employees are not in their offices at any one point in time.

◆ "Relatively little of the knowledge we possess as an organization is explicit – written down or in a knowledge base,"

Buckman says. "Our far greater share of knowledge is tacit – in the heads of our people."

◆ The prevalence of tacit knowledge suggested that "the ideal system of knowledge dissemination would be one in which we reduced the number of transmissions to one – from the person who had it to the person who needed it. That achieves the least distortion" – and points to the critical importance of empowerment.

Also required was a considerable ongoing investment in networking and communications technologies, to the tune of $7,500 per person per year. But the payoffs have been even more considerable. As Buckman recounts, "Our average global speed of response decreased from weeks, to days, to hours, then to minutes. We have no more corporate gatekeepers. We believe we are moving from the use of technology to control costs to the entrepreneurial application of technology to gain competitive advantage." One indicator of success in that effort: In less than 10 years, the company's sales from products that are less than five years old more than doubled, from 14 percent to 35 percent.[20]

"It's better to get a 10 percent increase in productivity from 20,000 employees than a 10 percent increase in productivity from the CEO."

John Chambers would not likely be surprised by such results, because he understands that, "If you empower employees by giving them access to the data, they will make decisions further down in the organization. It's better to get a 10 percent increase in productivity from 20,000 employees than a 10 percent increase in productivity from the CEO."[19]

USE THE NET TO REVOLUTIONIZE INTERNAL OPERATIONS

To fully exploit the Internet's virtually unlimited advantages, don't just look outward. Within your organization are long-standing functions and systems that can be approached in whole new ways when you apply a digital e-valuation of how things get done:

◆ **Turn information systems into a competitive advantage.** If it's true – as it has long been asserted – that information is power, then today's technologies can make information a superpower. You can use the Inter-net's capabilities to deliver more accurate and detailed information to more managers more quickly than ever before.

◆ **Hire better-faster-cheaper with the Web.** Cisco and other smart, talent-hungry companies have changed the face of staff recruiting by ex-ploiting the Internet. Done right – as Cisco has – Internet-based hiring can deliver better people, more quickly, with significant savings in re-cruiting costs. With today's ever-mounting talent crunch, you're well advised to make the most of Net staffing.

◆ **Hop aboard the e-train.** There is possibly no other business activity better suited for the Internet's inherent capabilities than employee train-ing. With the Net, you can cost-effectively pare the most nettlesome and costly problems of training – such as keeping content up to date – to relatively minor concerns.

◆ **Become an e-learning organization.** Knowledge sharing has never been more important than it is in our emerging knowledge economy – or more possible than it is by employing modern information technology. But an essential antecedent to knowledge sharing is a Cisco-like com-mitment to employee empowerment. Companies can no longer afford to have all information roads lead through their top ranks.

NOTES

1. Ignatius, David, "Online in the New Economy," *Washington Post,* 11 July 1999.

2. Sidener, Jonathan, "Cisco Systems Executive Discusses Internet's

Impact on World Economy," *Arizona Republic*, 24 September 1999, and Useem, Jerry, "For Sale Online: You," *Fortune*, 5 July 1999.

3. Neff, Thomas J., and Citrin, James M., *Lessons From the Top: The Search for America's Best Business Leaders*, Currency-Doubleday, New York, 1999.

4. Sidener, Jonathan, "Cisco Systems Executive Discusses Internet's Impact on World Economy," *Arizona Republic*, 24 September 1999.

5. Jones, Del, and Belton, Beth, "Cisco Chief: Virtual Close to Hit Big," *USA Today*, 12 October 1999.

6. Drucker, Peter F., *Management Challenges for the 21st Century*, HarperBusiness, New York, 1999.

7. Useem, Jerry, "For Sale Online: You," *Fortune*, 5 July 1999.

8. Useem, Jerry, "For Sale Online: You," *Fortune*, 5 July 1999.

9. Michael, Karine, "Go Online for Job," *[Durham, North Carolina] Herald-Sun*, 12 September 1999.

10. Port, Otis, "Customers Move Into the Driver's Seat," *Business Week*, 4 October 1999.

11. Useem, Jerry, "For Sale Online: You," *Fortune*, 5 July 1999.

12. Useem, Jerry, "For Sale Online: You," *Fortune*, 5 July 1999.

13. Cisco corporate news release, 3 November 1999.

14. Gillooly, Caryn, "Tech Companies Want Everything on the Web," *InternetWeek*, 27 September 1999.

15. Cisco corporate news release, 3 November 1999.

16. Port, Otis, "Customers Move Into the Driver's Seat," *Business Week*, 4 October 1999.

17. Author interview.

18. Presentation at International Strategic Leadership Forum, New York, April 1998.

19. Jones, Del, and Belton, Beth, "Cisco Chief: Virtual Close to Hit Big," *USA Today*, 12 October 1999.

Four

PUT PEOPLE BEFORE PRODUCTS, PROFITS, AND EVERYTHING ELSE

IN THIS CHAPTER

How do Cisco and a few other firms get and keep the best people? *Business Week*'s John Byrne has perhaps provided the best short answer: "They restore meaning to the Dilbert-scorned rhetoric that 'people are our most important assets.' The best of the Internet age breed [are] setting new standards for how to attract, cultivate, and retain talent in an era in which people matter more than ever." This chapter tells how Cisco makes that happen.

When Cisco Systems shops for acquisitions, as it has continuously for the six-year period in which it bought some 40 companies, its foremost consideration isn't products, or profits, or projected growth. "The key to our success is understanding that we are acquiring people, not technology," says executive VP Don Listwin.[1]

John Chambers elaborates: "When we acquire a company, we aren't simply acquiring its current products, we're acquiring the next generation of products through its people." Chambers says gauging the success of acquisitions is "real simple." You look at "retention of people and revenue that you generate two or three years later."[2]

By both measures, Cisco is possibly the most successful big company ever. A big part of the reason is that Cisco's concern for employees only begins with acquisition or hiring. It permeates the company – and shows up in numbers that have lots to do with profitability. To cite just one, for now: annual turnover is about 7 percent, the company says, versus an industry-wide average of 18 percent.[3]

SEEK PEOPLE WHO ARE MORE THAN SATISFACTORY

"As a leader, I am most proud of how broad and deep our team is," says John Chambers. "We've been able to get the top 10 percent to 15 percent of the people in the industry and have been able to motivate them to play together as a team."

Cisco has done this by looking for people in every likely nook and cranny. The company is said to have augmented its efforts at job fairs and over the Internet (described in the previous chapter) with recruiting at the Los Altos Wine & Art Festival and the Santa Clara Home & Garden Show, and also by placing a mobile billboard along some of Silicon Valley's most congested freeway stretches, suggesting that work at Cisco could reduce arduous commuting.[4]

Such creativity in recruiting by Cisco and other high-tech firms isn't a choice, but a necessity. A *Wall Street Journal* article reported on an Internet start-up's CEO who "spends about two-thirds of his time hunting new hires . . . backed by a recruitment team bigger than his marketing staff." His commitment "highlights how far businesses of all sizes must go to find talent in today's tight job market."[5]

Your company may not yet – or ever – have to recruit that extensively, but demographics and employment statistics suggest that the market for top talent is more likely to get tighter over time than to ease. So you may be well advised to consider adopting some of the recruiting strategies that have proven effective at high-tech firms such as Cisco – and Microsoft, which – according to author Randall E. Stross – "has pursued the best more successfully than other companies, and has visibly reaped the rewards more dramatically than others, too." In his book *The Microsoft Way*, Stross lists these key components of Microsoft's recruiting success:

◆ *Look beyond resumes.* Stross says Microsoft managers assume the best people aren't even looking.

◆ *Favor smarts over experience.* A record of previous relevant work may not be as reliable an indicator of future success as pure brainpower.

◆ *Seek very specific talents.* Microsoft wants a particular kind of smart person, someone who is "pragmatically inclined, verbally agile, and able to respond deftly when challenged." Also, recognizing the "rapid perishability" of today's knowledge, Microsoft goes for those with "the capability of grasping new knowledge extremely quickly, of generating acute questions on the spot, of perceiving connections between disparate domains of knowledge."

◆ *Get into the trenches when necessary.* Bill Gates himself will at times interview prospective candidates at levels below those of his direct reports, and is reported to be "ready to drop other matters and make a helpful call to a prospective star."

◆ *Prefer an open slot to a near fit.* In a company video on hiring, Gates says, "If you have somebody who's mediocre . . . we're really in big trouble." So Microsoft recruiters don't settle for "second best or a near fit, even if a continuing vacancy creates hardship."[6]

FIND PEOPLE WHO FIT YOUR CULTURE

John Chambers wants his employees' personal goals to align with Cisco's culture – for the employees' sake: "It's a shame for the company to succeed and yet have members of the company not achieve their personal goals. So we try to align the goals of the company with the goals of the individual."[7]

It certainly cascades into Cisco's acquisitions. In fact, Chambers indicates Cisco's unique culture practically *requires* acquisitions: "From the beginning we built a culture that wanted people from different environments and different backgrounds. There is no mold here. This is a culture that accepts outsiders with the realization that brainpower is what counts, and if you can get brainpower that fits into your culture, that's how you win."

Chambers' views on culture would be heartily endorsed by hiring and retention consultant Jim Harris, who asserts that "culture fit" is more important for keeping great employees than is "job fit." Not that job fit isn't important, he explains, "It's a minimum requirement for companies to be able to find and keep good employees." But culture fit, he adds, "determines whether someone is highly likely to remain with and be successful with the company." In this regard, Cisco outshines just about every company anywhere.

> **"This is a culture that accepts outsiders with the realization that brainpower is what counts."**

Harris and staffing consultant Joan Brannick, coauthors of *Finding & Keeping Great Employees*, say that Cisco is an excellent example of a company that excels at finding and keeping superior workers through a culture of innovation. They identify four forms of core culture:

◆ *Innovation* – where the focus is on new products, new markets, and new niches in existing markets. Example: Cisco.

◆ *Customer service* – where competitive advantage is gained through customer contact and building repeat business. Example: Home Depot.

◆ *Operational excellence* – the foundation of which is "to constantly improve systems, procedures, and product or service quality." Example: McDonald's.

◆ *Spirit* – where excellence is achieved by "unleashing people's limitless energy, creativity, and enthusiasm." Example: Chick-fil-A.[8]

Harris emphasizes that none of these culture types is superior to another and that characteristics of all four cultures will be found within most companies. "My key point is that superb companies will clearly emphasize one of these four forms of culture, and that this emphasis will show in staffing and retention practices that are aligned with the core culture."

The first step in achieving alignment is to identify which form of culture is core to the company. Among techniques Harris recommends is compiling a "great employee" profile. "Look at the top 10 percent of performers across all departments. I guarantee you'll find common traits that will help indicate your core driver."

Next, examine all of your staffing and retention practices in terms of how well they support the core culture, and emphasize those that do so most strongly. For example, Harris notes that a spirit-driven company may do well to offer sabbaticals, so employees can give time to civic and charitable groups. Practices should not be exclusively aimed at supporting the core culture. "We've found that an ideal level might be having about half of all practices support the core driver," Harris says.

When the core culture is identified and practices are aligned, "you'll see job candidates self-select to match your culture. If the company is service driven, for example, folks who are innovation driven will tend to go elsewhere." On the retention side, "Some people will leave the company – those who perform best in cultures that aren't the core driver for your company. Ultimately, that's best for the company and the worker."[9]

HOW CISCO KEEPS "ACQUIRED" EMPLOYEES

Cisco's success at holding on to employees gained through the company's acquisition of 40-plus companies since 1995 is nothing short of spectacular. Turnover among acquired employees is lower for Cisco than for its overall industry by a factor of 10.[10] How does Cisco get "acquirees" to stay?

◆ *It starts with letting them know they're wanted.* "It's important to give people in acquired companies bigger jobs, not smaller jobs," says executive VP Don Listwin. *Business Week* reports that three of Cisco's business groups are led by former CEOs of acquired companies.[11]

◆ *Acquirees can't easily lose those jobs.* Termination of any employee recently arrived from an acquired company requires consent of both Chambers and the former CEO. "It tells new employees that Cisco wants them, that Cisco cares about them, and that we're not just another big company," says legal and government affairs VP Daniel Scheinman. "It buys the trust of the people . . . and their passion is worth a lot more than any of the downside legal protection."[12]

◆ *They're tempted and retained with stock.* Most acquired employees see the Cisco shares they receive on acquisition double in value before they see the first anniversary of their employment.[13] An electrical engineer who came to Cisco by way of acquisition admitted that, because of his considerable accumulated wealth in the form of options, "I can't walk away, because I have a lot at stake with Cisco right now. The golden handcuffs really do work."[14]

TREAT PEOPLE LIKE PRECIOUS ASSETS (THEY ARE)

John Chambers is fond of telling interviewers that managing people isn't all that difficult, it's simply a matter of following the golden rule: "treating other people as you like to be treated."[15] Based on so many employers' less-than-stellar ability to keep good people, the golden rule seems not to be practiced widely. And with Cisco's less-than-peak salaries, employees are clearly attracted by something more than paychecks.[16] A review of company publications and reports by independent media reveals these top employee attractions:

◆ *Ownership.* "People used to work for wages," Chambers observes. "In the new economy, they work for ownership. Security comes from the stock."[17] And it's come in abundance for Cisco employees at all levels of the company. Chambers says that 40 percent of all employee stock options go to non-management employees and the "average individual contributor – not manager, not VP, not president – has over $250,000 in stock appreciation." It's reported that more than 2,000 of Cisco's employees are millionaires – based only on the value of their Cisco holdings.[18]

> "People used to work for wages. In the new economy, they work for ownership."

◆ *Belonging.* One-third or more of all Cisco employees arrived via acquisition – and is treated in a most extraordinary way (see sidebar).[19] Cisco launches a phalanx of inducements designed not just to keep people, but make acquisition a career highlight.

◆ *Having a say.* Cisco seeks input from employees at all levels. Among the more innovative channels is Chambers' monthly birthday breakfasts. All employees celebrating a birthday each month are invited to attend and say what they will to the CEO.[20] And criticism isn't discouraged. As Chambers puts it: "If you say you want risk takers and the first time somebody reports a problem, you shoot the person, then you're not going to get the information."[21]

◆ *Security.* Once forced as a manager at Wang to lay off some 5,000 employees in one fell swoop, Chambers today will go to almost any lengths to avoid such dismissals. He tells employees, "I'd rather have a little bit of stress on each of us than you be worried about your job."[22]

◆ *Egalitarianism.* Chambers doesn't care for perks conferred on select employees. "In our culture, we're all equals," he says. So there are no reserved parking spaces in company lots, members of the top team work out of the same size offices as other executives, and the company pays only for coach seating for anyone's business travel.[23]

◆ *Empowerment.* Incidents abound of below-top-rank Cisco employees having the wherewithal to push through important corporate initiatives. For example, Cisco's breakthrough uses of the Internet to sell its wares and handle customer service both originated from employee skunkworks set up by department heads. They rounded up a couple of engineers, worked on a shoestring, and were given the opportunity to present their proposals to top executives.[24]

◆ *Learning.* A report based on employee opinion gathered by

Vault.com, an online publisher of "insider" guides to workplaces, says Cisco people "laud the company's 'incredible' training program and enjoy the opportunity to 'work for a company where intelligence, learning aptitude, and resourcefulness are more highly prized than the ability to kiss butt.' . . . If working for one of the most powerful high-tech companies in the world in a fast-paced, learning-rich environment appeals to you, then Cisco Systems is the place to be."[25]

> Cisco people "laud the company's 'incredible' training program and enjoy the opportunity to 'work for a company where intelligence, learning aptitude, and resourcefulness are more highly prized than the ability to kiss butt.'"
>
> – Vault.com

Stanford Graduate School of Business professor Jeffrey Pfeffer is a strong advocate of measures, such as Cisco's, that put people first. "But implementing these ideas in a systematic, consistent fashion," he observes, "remains rare enough to be an important source of competitive advantage for firms in a number of industries."

Pfeffer, author of *The Human Equation: Building Profits by Putting People First*, charges that:

> . . . most companies say one thing, but then implement management practices that treat people as costs to be reduced, or as employees who can't be trusted and who need to be closely controlled. . . . If a company doesn't build a management system around a primary focus on people, then simply saying people are important means nothing.

To launch a corporate effort that puts people first, Pfeffer says,

A good start would be determining how well your company measures up against [practices] that seem to characterize most if not all companies which profit through people. [Then] start budgeting time to make people important. Installing a management system like this is hard work, but the payoff that comes from investing in people can be tremendous.[26]

PROVIDE A SETTING FOR SUPERB PERFORMANCE

John Chambers understands the importance of work conditions and environment to productivity, as he indicated in saying that one of four key determinants of company success today is attracting and keeping the best employee talent. "This is an area where a handful of really bright engineers will outproduce 1,000 engineers. We see that again and again. Now, we're trying to get that handful of really bright people in every functional group and then empower them and keep them."[27]

"A handful of really bright engineers will outproduce 1,000 engineers. We see that again and again."

As Chambers knows, and experts increasingly affirm, salary alone is no longer the way to attract and keep really bright people. One of these experts, Karl Erik Sveiby, claims that organizations are increasingly valued as much or more for their intangible assets as for their tangible assets. In his book *The New Organizational Wealth: Managing and Measuring Knowledge-Based Assets*, Sveiby notes that a unique set of managerial skills is required to successfully manage a "high-intangibles" unit of an organization, particularly one stocked with professionals. Among the ways he recommends "to foster the conditions under which professionals can be most creative":

◆ *Help them feel secure.* Boost professionals' confidence in their ability to deal effectively with whatever lies ahead.

◆ *Avoid vertical division of labor.* Professionals "loath routine tasks." Help them cope, by minimizing routine tasks and fairly dividing those that remain.

◆ *Motivate with intangible rewards* – such as peer recognition, learning opportunities, and opportunities for more independence. Devise compensation that is based less on fixed salary than on "value added."

◆ *Provide alternatives to plateauing.* Find new duties – such as mentor, teacher, salesperson, ambassador – for professionals who reach "creative plateaus."[28]

SOME WAYS TO REGISTER CISCO-LIKE RETENTION[29]

Cisco's annual employee attrition averages only 7 percent – less than half the rate for the overall IT industry. If you'd like to achieve Cisco's incredible retention rate in your unit, but figure the measures to make it happen must be issued from on high, here's some good news: Organizational development consultants Beverly Kaye and Sharon Jordan-Evans asked more than 3,000 people from diverse jobs and industries to list the top three to five reasons they chose to stay with a single employer for periods of two years or more. The most common reasons, reported in their book *Love 'Em or Lose 'Em: Getting Good People to Stay*, are listed here in order of their overall popularity and frequency:

1. Career growth, learning, and development

2. Exciting and challenging work

3. Meaningful work – making a difference and a contribution

(Note: 90 percent of respondents listed at least one of the first three items among the top three or four reasons they stay.)

4. Great people

5. Being part of a team

6. Good boss

7. Recognition for work well done

8. Fun on the job

9. Autonomy – sense of control over my work

10. Flexibility, including work hours and dress code

(Note: All 10 of the reasons listed above are more important for retention than is pay.)

11. Fair pay and competitive benefits

12. Inspiring leadership

KISS NONPERFORMERS GOODBYE

Cisco's incredibly low annual employee turnover is even more impressive considering that about half of those who leave the company do so involuntarily. They're dismissed as part of company policy to show the exit to the bottom 5 percent of performers each year. Human resources VP Barbara Beck says, "The decision of who to let go has nothing to do with length of service or level. It's 'are you adding value?' or 'do you fit the culture?'"[30]

Because John Chambers publicly acknowledges his admiration of General Electric CEO Jack Welch, it seems likely that Cisco's policy of forced attrition is modeled on Welch's similar effort at GE, where the legendary leader insists on hiring only the best. At a meeting of GE's top executives, for example, Welch is reported to have requested that any "C-level performer" be shown a pink slip and the nearest exit. GE, he said, is an A-plus company.[31]

> "The decision of who to let go has nothing to do with length of service or level. It's 'are you adding value?' or 'do you fit the culture?'" – Cisco HR VP Barbara Beck

Getting rid of people who are less than superb contributors is part of a hiring and development system dubbed "topgrading" by its originator, consultant Bradford D. Smart. "Winning in today's talent-driven information age depends on packing your organization with 'A' players and clearing out the 'C' players," says Smart, who wrote *Topgrading*. Smart defines A players as the top 10 percent of talent available for a position. B players are those among the next 25 percent of available talent. Those rated C fall anywhere below the top 35 percent.

Smart says topgrading involves:

◆ proactively searching out and identifying A players,

◆ providing for all employees the coaching necessary to become and remain A players, and

◆ redeploying chronic C players into either internal positions where they can be A players or outside the company.

So would the nation's unemployment rolls swell with millions of non-A players if every organization used Smart's topgrading system? "Not at all," he responds. "Everyone is a B or C player in some jobs – but is also an A player in other jobs. The key is for everyone to find an A slot, whether by choice or by being redeployed from a topgrading company."[32]

PUT PEOPLE BEFORE PRODUCTS, PROFITS, AND EVERYTHING ELSE

There's more than a magnanimous gesture in a company's commitment to putting its people first. That's because everything else an organization values – its products, profits, and so forth – flows from its people. John Chambers is publicly recognized for a commitment to employees that may be unsurpassed among today's CEOs. His guiding principles can be yours, too:

◆ **Seek people who are more than satisfactory.** With price and product-quality differentiations among competitors gradually disappearing, the key basis of competition is increasingly the talent of employees. That means a job candidate who is merely qualified to fill your open slot may no longer suffice; you've got to attract and hire the person who's perfect for the job.

◆ **Find people who fit your culture.** Because corporate culture is increasingly important for long-term corporate success, it's increasingly important to hire people who provide not just job fit, but culture fit as well. The payoff, as Cisco clearly demonstrates, is a corps of employees whose personal aims are aligned with corporate aims.

◆ **Treat people like precious assets (they are).** Cisco says its employees are the company's most highly prized assets. Unlike too many other employers, the company backs its assertion with actions: pay, empowerment, and a host of other expressions that its people are the ultimate source of corporate success.

◆ **Provide a setting for superb performance.** With unprecedented demand for good employees, particularly managers and professionals, companies like Cisco understand it takes more than traditional inducements to retain top performers. Also required are intangibles such as intellectually challenging assignments and a high-energy working environment.

◆ **Kiss nonperformers goodbye.** Despite record demand for good workers, you can strive to continually upgrade the overall quality of your employees by dismissing your poorest performers. That forces the ongoing company recruitment effort into overdrive; the payoff is new people who collectively outperform those let go.

NOTES

1. Port, Otis, "Customers Move Into the Driver's Seat," *Business Week*, 4 October 1999.

2. Daly, James, "The Art of the Deal," *Business 2.0*, October 1999.

3. Reinhardt, Andy, "The Man Who Hones Cisco's Cutting Edge, *Business Week*, 13 September 1999.

4. Port, Otis, "Customers Move Into the Driver's Seat," *Business Week*, 4 October 1999.

5. Lublin, Joann S., "An E-Company CEO Is Also the Recruiter-in-Chief," *Wall Street Journal*, 9 November 1999.

6. Stross, Randall E., *The Microsoft Way*, Addison-Wesley, Cambridge, Massachusetts, 1996.

7. Daly, James, "The Art of the Deal," *Business 2.0*, October 1999.

8. Harris, Jim, and Brannick, Joan, *Finding & Keeping Great Employees*, Amacom, New York, 1999.

9. Author interview.

10. Goldblatt, Henry, "Cisco's Secrets," *Fortune*, 8 November 1999.

11. Byrne, John, "The Corporation of the Future," *Business Week*, 24 August 1998.

12. Byrne, John, "The Corporation of the Future," *Business Week*, 24 August 1998.

13. Holson, Laura M., "Whiz Kid: Young Deal Maker Is the Force Behind a Company's Growth," *New York Times*, 19 November 1998.

14. Anderson, Mark, "Ascent of the Nerd," *National Post*, 1 October 1999.

15. ABC-TV, "20/20," September 15, 1999, and Neff, Thomas J., and Citrin, James M., *Lessons From the Top: The Search for America's Best Business Leaders*, Currency-Doubleday, New York, 1999.

16. Vault.com corporate news release, 17 September 1999.

17. Port, Otis, "Customers Move Into the Driver's Seat," *Business Week*, 4 October 1999.

18. ABC-TV, "20/20," 15 September 1999.

19. Port, Otis, "Customers Move Into the Driver's Seat," *Business Week*, 4 October 1999.

20. Byrne, John, "The Corporation of the Future," *Business Week*, 24 August 1998.

21. Jones, Del, and Belton, Beth, "Cisco Chief: Virtual Close to Hit Big," *USA Today*, 12 October 1999.

22. ABC-TV, "20/20," 15 September 1999.

23. ABC-TV, "20/20," 15 September 1999.

24. Tully, Shawn, "How Cisco Mastered the Net," *Fortune*, 17 August 1998.

25. Vault.com corporate news release, 17 September 1999.

26. Author interview.

27. Daly, James, "The Art of the Deal," *Business 2.0*, October 1999.

28. Sveiby, Karl Erik, *The New Organizational Wealth: Managing and Measuring Knowledge-Based Assets*, Berrett-Koehler, San Francisco, 1997.

29. Kaye, Beverly, and Jordan-Evans, Sharon, *Love Em or Lose Em: Getting Good People to Stay*, Berrett-Koehler, San Francisco, 1999.

30. Port, Otis, "Customers Move Into the Driver's Seat," *Business Week*, 4 October 1999.

31. Swoboda, Frank, "Talking Management With Chairman Welch," *Washington Post*, 23 March 1997.

32. Author interview.

Five

LISTEN CONSTANTLY TO CUSTOMERS

IN THIS CHAPTER

Consider this statement from Cisco's annual report: "Cisco's number one priority and passion continues to be customer focus." How many corporate annual reports make a similar claim? Thousands? For how many of those companies would the claim be true? The central importance of the customer, according to *Business Week*'s John Byrne, is "another theme, often heard but seldom exercised by corporate leaders."[1] But in Cisco's case, Byrne acknowledges, the theme is exercised to an extent matched by few, if any, other firms. This chapter reveals how Cisco does it – and you can, too.

Johm Chambers grasps both the critical importance of customer focus and the fact that it is often preached and seldom practiced: "Customer satisfaction is so critical. I learned that the hard way at IBM and Wang. And you watch what happened to DEC or Apple Computer. When their customer satisfaction dropped, 12 to 24 months later, their revenues dropped. So there is a one-to-one correlation that corporate America doesn't pay attention to as it should."[2]

Chambers is also among the still-few corporate leaders who both understands and responds effectively to the emerging effects of the Internet on the customer–supplier relationship: the Internet gives customers the upper hand to a far greater extent than ever before. Sandra Vandermerwe, management chair at the Imperial College, London, explains in her book *Customer Capitalism* that customers now exercise increasing power because, "for the first time, technology allows them to talk to each other. As more customers go online and chat, the firm becomes more transparent and less able to control its image or influence by traditional marketing means."[3]

Business Week's Otis Port sees the buyer's new power as "a Copernican revolution of sorts," in which "the customer is becoming the center of the entire business universe."[4] Under Chambers, Cisco has customers firmly fixed at the center.

MAKE CUSTOMER SERVICE HAPPEN: MEASURE IT, PAY FOR IT

Cisco is incessant in its drive to learn about its customers. John Chambers says, "We do surveys all the time, in terms of what's working or not, and we have about 70 different characteristics we look for in that survey."[5] When is "all the time"? Among other occasions, Chambers has specified that a measure or assessment of customer satisfaction follows "after every customer visit," is gathered as a means to "track every problem," and is reported directly to him to "review how well we are doing with every critical account every night."[6]

By continually asking customers what they think, Cisco avoids the pitfalls that often lay in assumptions – the subject of consultant Eileen Shapiro's book *How Corporate Truths Become Competitive Traps*. She notes that assuming rather than asking leads companies, "time and again," to "deliver product and service features consumers don't want, or benefits they don't value."[7] Similarly, consultant Earl Naumann, in his book *Creating Customer Value*, identifies "the gap between customer expectations and management's perception of those expectations" as a "service quality gap" that will occur when a company does little customer satisfaction research, when research results aren't integrated into decision making, or when managers assume what customers want without substantiation.[8]

The benefits of asking customers what they think go beyond the quantitative to the psychological. Consultant Ron Zemke, who heads Minneapolis-based Performance Research Associates, calls this the "nose-in-the-window" effect – named for an incident he witnessed when he accompanied a telephone company repair technician on customer calls. "At almost every stop, as the employee circled the property looking at poles and hook-ups, I could see the nose in the window: the customer watching every move the technician made. When I asked customers about their concern, every one of them said, 'I want to explain the problem.' The technician didn't need that information to make the repair, but it was a must to fix the customer."[9]

Measuring customer satisfaction is essential to learn what customers want, but it is only part of what's required to make superb customer service happen for a company. "If you really believe . . . customer satisfaction is the most important measure," Chambers observes, "then you've got to tie it to your reward system, to your management practices. And we do."[10] At Cisco, managers' annual bonuses are determined in part by the company's most comprehensive annual survey of customer satisfaction, in which business units are rated in a variety of measures on a scale of 1 to 5. The overall corporate goal for 2000 was a rating of 4.23, which Chambers terms "off the charts."[11]

> "If you really believe . . . customer satisfaction is the most important measure, then you've got to tie it to your reward system."

The overall effect of stressing customer satisfaction to the point of paying for it is pointedly summed up by a market research executive who says that Chambers has "done a really successful job of making everybody in the company think they're salespeople."[12]

HOW TO MAKE THE MOST OF CUSTOMER SURVEYS[14]

Marketing specialist and author Ros Jay agrees with John Chambers' contention that customer satisfaction is a company's most important measure. "That's the only measure that really, really counts," she writes. "All the others are simply ways of getting there more easily." Jay offers these suggestions for making customer surveys as accurate and informative as possible:

◆ Aim for a written response that takes 3–5 minutes to complete; for phone surveys, take no more than 10 minutes. Annual, in-depth surveys of big customers may be stretched to an hour.

◆ Ask a mix of questions, some of which are objective (generally reflect simple facts, e.g. "Did your delivery arrive on time?") and others that are subjective (generally require evaluation or opinion, e.g. "On a scale of 1–10, how would you rate the engineer's manner?").

◆ Make sure cumulative responses are easy to analyze with yes/no answers, multiple choice, scales of 1–10, and similar concrete methods.

◆ Report results of surveys at least monthly to keep in touch with customers' attitudes and how they change over time.

◆ Always be open to changing surveys to gain more meaningful information: continually ask customers informally what they think you should be asking, and periodically conduct formal surveys or focus groups to pinpoint suggested survey changes.

LET CUSTOMER WANTS SHAPE YOUR STRATEGY

Do you believe that customers have more clout than ever in determining the products, features, prices, and terms offered by the companies they buy from? Well, as Al Jolson said in the first-ever motion picture with sound: "You ain't heard nothin' yet!"

In the case of 21st century commerce, the reason that famous phrase applies can be stated in a word: Internet. As noted in a report by consultants Booz-Allen & Hamilton

> Companies are beginning to embrace the concept of Internet-enabled extended enterprise, where they work in concert with their constituencies electronically. The pay-offs can be tremendous: the Internet allows companies not only to align with their customers on order management, but also on product configuration and design, resulting in better customer services and more satisfied customers.[14]

Business Week sees the same transformation, but states its consequences in terms that are not so much opportunities as imperatives: "In this new model, strategic direction is not formed by an insular group of top executives, but by the company's leading customers."[15] A firm exemplifying the new approach, the magazine says, is Cisco. That was far from true, however, before John Chambers joined the company: "Cisco badly needed to improve relations with customers. Like many tech startups, the company had an engineering-driven culture where the needs of customers took a back seat to the coolest new technology."[16]

Chambers "flipped that relationship around," *Business Week* recounts.

> After Boeing Co. and Ford Motor Co. informed Chambers that their future network needs were unlikely to be satisfied by Cisco, Chambers went out to make his first acquisition to solve the problem. That deal, to acquire local-area-network switch-

maker Crescendo Communications in 1993, put the company into a sector of the industry that now accounts for $2.8 billion in annual revenue.[17]

More important, the acquisition illustrated the shape of things to come under Chambers – that Cisco would from then forward be shaped by customers to a startling extent:

◆ *In technology* – Unlike some Silicon Valley CEOs credited as visionaries in anticipating the technologies that change the terms of commerce and communication, Chambers is regarded by some as weak in identifying the defining technologies of the future[18] – and apparently not of a mind that personal adeptness would make much difference. "We have no religion when it comes to technology," he says. "If the customers say this is what they're going to do regardless of our engineering views on it, that's what we're going to help them do."[19]

◆ *In structure* – Chambers reports that in the 1990s, Cisco has been restructured seven times in its quest to stay as closely in touch with customer needs as possible.[20]

◆ *In direction* – "There is nothing more arrogant than telling a customer: 'Here is what you need to know,'" says Chambers. "Most of the time, you are not going to be right." So Cisco's leading-edge customers, according to *Business Week*, "are seen as partners in forming the company strategy."[21]

> **"There is nothing more arrogant than telling a customer: 'Here is what you need to know.'"**

If Chambers and his top team experience any lack of ego gratification in not emerging from an annual corporate retreat at a tony West Coast resort to issue *the* Cisco corporate strategy, they betray none of it to the many analysts and reporters who watch the company's every move. On the contrary, Chambers himself says, "If you ask what I'm most proud of, . . . [f]irst is our almost fanatical approach to customer success. We don't say it, we do it. . . . It's something I don't have to explain to anyone in our company anymore."[22]

> "If you ask what I'm most proud of . . . First is our almost fanatical approach to customer success. We don't say it, we do it."

IS THE CUSTOMER THE STRATEGY FOR YOUR FIRM?[23]

Has your company broadened its strategic planning process to include customer input? The way you answer the following questions may help you respond. They are drawn selectively from a longer list of questions that Arthur D. Little consultants Ronald S. Jonash and Tom Sommerlatte provide in their book *The Innovation Premium* to suggest how extensively a reader's company may be employing a "next-generation" innovation process.

◆ Do you value and manage external input from customers, industry colleagues, and competitors?

◆ Do you actively solicit input from these sources in developing new products and services?

◆ Does your company reward creative idea gathering, idea researching, and successful idea implementation?

◆ Do your scientists, inventors, engineers, and product creators mix with one another and share ideas with colleagues?

◆ What role do your customers play in product development? Is their input considered even before an idea is developed?

CISCO'S CHANNELS (CUSTOMER SEGMENTS)[24]

◆ *Service providers* – The outfits that sell transmission of voice, data, and/or video signals: Internet service providers, wireless and traditional telephone companies, cable systems. This segment accounts for about 30 percent of Cisco's revenue.

◆ *Telephone companies* – Some observers – such as analysts and research firms – distinguish between the historically voice-only phone companies (from what John Chambers calls the "old world") and the previously data-only Internet service providers (that operate in the "new world"). The distinction is important because it makes Cisco a bit player in sales to phone companies, with less than 1 percent of a $225 billion market.

◆ *Enterprises* – Big companies and organizations that need a broad variety of networking products and service (what Cisco and other technology firms call "end-to-end solutions") to link their own multiple and widespread locations and also – increasingly – tie into their major suppliers and customers. Cisco gets about half of its total revenue from this segment.

◆ *Small and medium businesses* – Most of the company's sales in this channel are made to "value-added resellers" – businesses once known as retailers, middlemen, and independent sales agents – that resell to small and mid-sized firms. The segment accounts for about 20 percent of Cisco revenue.

◆ *Consumers* – A relatively new segment for Cisco: individuals and families in their homes. Accounts for negligible Cisco revenue now, but could be worth billions in only a few years.

TAILOR OFFERINGS FOR DISCRETE SALES CHANNELS

(Note: The word 'channel,' as used within the IT industry, seems usually to refer to a segment of a market that is served through intermediaries; for example, Cisco sells to small and mid-sized businesses largely through resellers. This book uses 'channel' more broadly, as any sales avenue that links a seller and any group of customers that comprises a market segment for that seller – whether the link is direct or through intermediaries. As defined in the book Channel Champions, *"a channel is the essence of the way customers and a business interact . . . it is a business's route to its customers.")*[25]

The rise of the Internet as a global economic force entails, as discussed above, the rise of the customer to a position of unprecedented leverage with suppliers. Fortunately for the sellers, the Internet and its attendant technological advances also provide the means to respond effectively to these newly empowered customers – to address each customer's unique needs through products and services designed specifically for discrete channels.

But not many companies, other than standouts including Cisco, have yet begun to tailor their offerings to the extent possible and increasingly demanded by customers. Joel Friedman and Tony Laglinais of Andersen Consulting note that,

In many industries, individual companies still offer discrete products or services through physical distribution channels to a proprietary, undifferentiated clientele. Virtually overnight, however, the Internet and user-friendly technology have empowered a new generation of consumers who are challenging this long-accepted structure of commerce. The result is a fundamental shift from a seller-driven to a buyer-driven world.[26]

Cisco has responded with channel-specific marketing and partnering initiatives that go well beyond traditional incentives, such as win-lose price discounting, to win–win offerings that are not just creative, but also are aimed at winning customer loyalty and establishing long-term relationships. Particularly notable are the company's highly successful efforts aimed at the distributors and "value-added resellers" (VARs) who deal directly with end-customers in Cisco's small and medium businesses channel. According to an article in *Computer Reseller News*:

> . . . distributors and VARs alike are praising [Cisco's] strategy. . . . "Cisco is an example of all that is right and good," said Steve Raymund, chief executive of Tech Data Corp., Clearwater, Fla. . . . [Cisco] programs instantly reward VARs for their expertise and don't discourage them from entering the market against larger integrators that have larger volumes, [Cisco VP Tom] Stevenson said. . . . Analysts also praise Cisco for melding channel service and support with technology leadership to create a dominant brand.[27]

Cisco has similarly won rave reviews for its "Cisco Resource Network," described by the company as a means of providing small and mid-sized businesses with "information and tools to . . . learn about the Internet and connect with the right resources for complete installation and support."[29]

Those resources, of course, are the very resellers and others who powerfully affect end-customer choices of going with

Cisco or a competitor to meet networking needs. *InfoWorld* magazine related the experience of "one user, who used a pilot version of the Cisco Resource Network," for a complex installation that came off, in the end-customer's assessment, "without a hitch. . . . We . . . were not much involved, except to see that the service worked – from that context it's been absolutely marvelous."

One analyst said he believes Cisco is headed in the right direction. "It's a much more complex world than in the previous computing generation. You need enhanced support services, and Cisco recognizes that. . . . Cisco is providing the right set of channel support solutions and end-customer solutions with the certified partners, full access to configuration tools, and online support."[29]

> "It's a much more complex world than in the previous computing generation. You need enhanced support services, and Cisco recognizes that." – *InfoWorld* magazine

---

FIVE KEY STEPS TO SUPERIOR CHANNEL MANAGEMENT[31]

"Channel management is more than distribution or logistics," write Booz-Allen & Hamilton consultants Steven Wheeler and Evan Hirsh in their book *Channel Champions: How Leading Companies Build New Strategies to Serve Customers.* "It is a way of thinking, a way of making new connections with customers to exploit new commercial opportunities. . . . Effective channel management offers the chance to reinvent not just your business but the industry you're in." How do you make it happen? Wheeler and Hirsh list five basic steps:

1. *Understand customer buying and ownership needs and segments.* When you do, you can target particular groups of cus-

tomers with the aim of delivering the exactly right mix of products and services they value.

2. *Develop new channel concepts to capture both customer and product lifecycle value.* You segment so you can design different bundles of product attributes and associated services to match the needs and desires of different sets of consumers.

3. *Pilot test to refine the economics and competitive positioning of the channel concepts – structures, services, and operational systems.* This is primarily to minimize risk and refine the concepts before rollout.

4. *Rapidly roll out the concepts across segments and geographic territories.* When opening a new channel, being ahead of competitors can transform the market . . . especially when you gain one-to-one customer relationships.

5. *Study the results and adapt your channel.* Failure to do so will erode the channel offering over time. Channel management is a continuous process.

MAINTAIN TOP-DOWN DIRECT, PERSONAL CUSTOMER CONTACT

John Chambers and other members of Cisco's top management team let nothing stand in the way of their continuing direct contact with customers – not the company's astounding growth, not their own expanding areas of responsibility, not even their scheduled meetings with shareholders, directors, and world leaders. Here are selected snapshots that illustrate their commitment to staying close to customers:

◆ Chambers was 20 minutes late for his first board meeting as CEO because he was on the phone with a distraught user. "The board members were not happy campers when I arrived," Chambers says. "But when I told them why, they said I could use that excuse anytime."[31]

◆ Chambers spends more than half of his time with customers; every night, 365 nights a year, he receives voice mail updates on as many as 15 key clients.[32]

◆ Cisco maintains a "Critical Accounts" list. Customers can put themselves on this watch list and get instant, daily attention from top management.[33]

◆ When cable Internet service provider Excite@Home had just six employees in 1995, Chambers himself showed up to pitch the business – which left the acting CEO "stunned." Later, when Excite@Home gave some of its business to rival Bay Networks, Chambers came back and offered the startup the same terms Cisco gave its biggest clients – and ended up with all the business.[34]

When Excite@Home gave some of its business to rival Bay Networks, Chambers came back and offered the startup the same terms Cisco gave its biggest clients – and ended up with all the business.

◆ At a lavish event for customers in December 1998, Chambers focused particular attention on the CIO of UAL (parent of United Airlines). "Chambers won't give up," the CIO says.[35]

◆ With all customers, Chambers gives out his personal phone number and urges them to call anytime. "He'll take a phone call at 2 a.m.," says Cisco executive VP Gary Daichendt.[36]

LISTEN CONSTANTLY TO CUSTOMERS

In an Internet-enabled world, where buyers have instant access to products and services offered by a world of providers, the customer is more powerful – and less loyal – than ever before. Cisco has rocketed to unprecedented success on the strength of its obsessive customer concern, which is no more evident than in John Chambers himself. He leads by example, as you can, too, observing these key tenets of customer focus:

◆ **Make customer service happen: measure it, pay for it.** Don't pretend to know what customers want. Instead, ask them – in formal surveys and informal conversation – and follow up with offerings that precisely respond to customer wishes. Then elevate customer service from talk to commitment by tying it to employee compensation.

◆ **Let customer wants shape your strategy.** Customers are more than end users for Cisco; they're integral to shaping the company's strategy and operations. That model of customer involvement will be increasingly prevalent in the 21st century, as corporate success hinges more than ever on perceiving and acting on changing customer needs.

◆ **Tailor offerings for discrete sales channels.** As yet, only a few stellar companies such as Cisco have structured product and service offerings to the specific needs of specific markets. But solutions tailored to discrete channels will become the norm as competition weeds out companies that cling to an outmoded one-size-fits-all mentality.

◆ **Maintain top-down direct, personal customer contact.** There's no substitute for the voice of the customer, direct and unfiltered by any intermediary's report. You've got to spend time with customers, and in the process impress the central importance of the customer on everyone in your organization.

NOTES

1. Byrne, John, "The Corporation of the Future," *Business Week*, 24 August 1998.

2. Daly, James, "The Art of the Deal," *Business 2.0*, October 1999.

3. Vandermerwe, Sandra, *Customer Capitalism*, Nicholas Brealey, Naperville, Illinois, 1999.

4. Port, Otis, "Customers Move Into the Driver's Seat," *Business Week*, 4 October 1999.

5. Daly, James, "The Art of the Deal," *Business 2.0*, October 1999.

6. Neff, Thomas J., and Citrin, James M., *Lessons From the Top: The Search for America's Best Business Leaders*, Currency-Doubleday, New York, 1999.

7. Shapiro, Eileen, *How Corporate Truths Become Competitive Traps*, John Wiley & Sons, New York, 1992.

8. Naumann, Earl, *Creating Customer Value*, Thompson Executive Press, Cincinnati, 1995.

9. Author interview

10. Neff, Thomas J., and Citrin, James M., *Lessons From the Top: The Search for America's Best Business Leaders*, Currency-Doubleday, New York, 1999.

11. Daly, James, "The Art of the Deal," *Business 2.0*, October 1999.

12. Reinhardt, Andy, "The Man Who Hones Cisco's Cutting Edge," *Business Week*, 13 September 1999.

13. Jay, Ros, *Smart Things to Know About Customers*, Capstone, Oxford, 1999.

14. Taylor, Paul, "Online Revolution Set to Overthrow Many Established Practices, *Financial Times*, 19 July 1999.

15. Byrne, John, "The Corporation of the Future," *Business Week*, 24 August 1998.

16. Reinhardt, Andy, "The Man Who Hones Cisco's Cutting Edge," *Business Week*, 13 September 1999.

17. Byrne, John, "The Corporation of the Future," *Business Week*, 24 August 1998.

18. Reinhardt, Andy, "The Man Who Hones Cisco's Cutting Edge," *Business Week*, 13 September 1999.

19. Neff, Thomas J., and Citrin, James M., *Lessons From the Top: The Search for America's Best Business Leaders*, Currency-Doubleday, New York, 1999.

20. Van, Jon, "Cisco Chief: Prepare For Internet Changes," *Chicago Tribune*, 1 October 1999.

21. Byrne, John, "The Corporation of the Future," *Business Week*, 24 August 1998.

22. Neff, Thomas J., and Citrin, James M., *Lessons From the Top: The Search for America's Best Business Leaders*, Currency-Doubleday, New York, 1999.

23. Jonash, Ronald S., and Sommerlatte, Tom, *The Innovation Premium: How Next-Generation Companies Are Achieving Peak Performance and Profitability*, Perseus, Cambridge, Massachusetts, 1999.

24. Cisco corporate Website; Ries, Al, and Kinni, Theodore B., *Future Focus*, Capstone, Oxford, 2000; and Reinhardt, Andy, "Mr. Internet," *Business Week*, 13 September 1999.

25. Wheeler, Steven, and Hirsh, Evan, *Channel Champions*, Jossey-Bass, San Francisco, 1999.

26. Taylor, Paul, "Online Revolution Set to Overthrow Many Established Practices, *Financial Times*, 19 July 1999.

27. Zarley, Craig, and Semilof, Margie, "The Cisco Kid – the Networking Giant Is Winning Friends in the Channel," *Computer Reseller News*, 13 September 1999.

28. Cisco 1999 corporate annual report.

29. Holt, Stannie, and Kujubu, Laura, "Cisco Teams with Vendors to Be E-commerce Resource," *InfoWorld Daily News,* 3 August 1999.

30. Wheeler, Steven, and Hirsh, Evan, *Channel Champions*, Jossey-Bass, San Francisco, 1999.

31. Reinhardt, Andy, "The Man Who Hones Cisco's Cutting Edge," *Business Week*, 13 September 1999.

32. Byrne, John, "The Corporation of the Future," *Business Week*, 24 August 1998.

33. Ignatius, David, "Online in the New Economy," *Washington Post*, 11 July 1999.

34. Reinhardt, Andy, "The Man Who Hones Cisco's Cutting Edge," *Business Week*, 13 September 1999.

35. Reinhardt, Andy, "The Man Who Hones Cisco's Cutting Edge," *Business Week*, 13 September 1999.

36. Reinhardt, Andy, "The Man Who Hones Cisco's Cutting Edge," *Business Week*, 13 September 1999.

Six

SERVE YOUR CORE CUSTOMERS FROM START TO END-TO-END

IN THIS CHAPTER

Cisco Systems – from its hardly threatening early days when company founders and friends assembled a single product, routers, on a living room floor – has rocketed to a dominance of the Internet networking equipment industry that is Microsoft-like in its proportions. Analysts estimate that more than 80 percent of Internet traffic flows over Cisco gear at some point.[1] This chapter reveals the keys to Cisco's ascent from single-product provider to supplier of end-to-end networking solutions.

John Chambers is unabashed in stating his desire to make Cisco *the* end-to-end provider (singular) of Internet-related products and services. "By providing the end-to-end network plumbing," he says, "we can change the way entire companies and industries operate."[2] He seems to be succeeding: as *PC Week* observes, "Cisco has risen to a dominance rivaled only by Microsoft Corp. and Intel Corp. among computing powerhouses."[3]

That's all well and good, from Cisco's perspective, when looking at the history of Internet networking to date. But Cisco has only recently embarked on its biggest-ever battle for end-to-end dominance: the fight for supremacy in the "converged" market of data, voice, and video transmission. Here, Cisco is matched against stellar companies, including a couple that are bigger – Lucent Technologies and Nortel Networks. Chambers and his team will have to pay close attention to the lessons from Cisco's own experience to again gain end-to-end market dominance.

BE EVERYTHING YOUR CUSTOMERS NEED . . .

John Chambers is acclaimed for knowing what customers want. And one of their foremost wants today is fewer suppliers. "Customers don't want more vendors in their network or environment, they want fewer," he says. "So you have to align, based on how customers are purchasing."[4]

It's unlikely that any other big company is as aligned with customers as Cisco is. The company "has the broadest and deepest product portfolio in the industry," says CS First Boston analyst Paul Weinstein.[5] A key customer confirms that assessment: "Cisco is positioned to serve both sides of the market – enterprises and service providers – better than anyone else," says Bob Pinney, a senior network engineer at Turner Broadcasting System Inc. According to *Information Week*, Turner's 200-site worldwide network "is almost entirely a Cisco shop."[6]

Chambers' conviction to make Cisco be everything his customers want in the way of Internet networking opens a broad avenue of continuing growth for the company. An article in *Harvard Management Update* notes that "a large company has only three paths to rapid growth." It can participate in a burgeoning industry, buy other firms, or do what it's already doing – "only somehow opening up whole new horizons." Cisco's hypergrowth flows from all three of these sources. This book addresses the first two elsewhere; here we consider the secrets of a "new-horizons" gambit.[7]

Opening whole new horizons requires a change of organizational mindset. Walt Disney Company, for example, grew sluggishly as a movie studio and theme park operator. But Michael Eisner shifted the mindset, seeing Disney as a company in the business of making people happy. Cisco has similarly shifted its corporate mindset, going from a provider of routers to Internet plumbers to the company that empowers "the Internet generation." What does Cisco sell under its current mindset? Whatever the Internet generation needs to be empowered. That's lots more than routers.

The Harvard article suggests three key steps to growth via whole new horizons:

Establish an explicit, visible growth portfolio. Your company should have business units at various stages of growth and maturity. The more established ones can generate the cash necessary to fund growth of the others. Units in their adolescence should be capable of growing fast in the near term. And still others should be "new and experimental" – positioned to fuel growth in the out years. Cisco's (relatively) mature line of business – sales of core data networking equipment to big companies – effectively supports the company's current big push into telecommunications markets long dominated by Lucent and Nortel.

> "Cisco is positioned to serve both sides of the market – enterprises and service providers – better than anyone else." – Cisco customer Bob Pinney

2. *Protect the new ventures from their worst enemy – the organization.* Management procedures and controls that may be appropriate for mature units can be the death of infant enterprises. "That's why successful growers cocoon their new businesses, separating them structurally or geographically from the rest of the corporation." (Cisco cocoons, in effect, through acquisitions and investments, discussed in Chapter 8.)

3. *Build growth into the company's DNA.* Corporate DNA comprises practices that are ingrained in – and inseparable from – the culture. A growth imperative must pervade that DNA – so the company will be genetically programmed to respond to customers' every need. In this regard, it's

unlikely that any company's growth DNA is stronger or more prevalent than Cisco's.

. . . AND NO MORE THAN YOUR CUSTOMERS NEED

When it comes to giving customers what they need, end-to-end is one thing, open-ended is quite another. Recognize that Cisco is all things Internet, not all things to all people. The sad experience of 1970s-style conglomerations of unrelated lines of business, such as ITT, demonstrates the danger in losing corporate focus. In their book *Future Focus*, Al Ries and Theodore B. Kinni observe, "The Internet is enabled by the ability of networks to communicate with each other and, happily for Cisco, the company has spent its first 15 years firmly focused on the products that make that communication possible."[9]

Ries, probably the world's premier purveyor of the focus doctrine, illustrates the effectiveness of focus by asking what word comes to mind when you think about Domino's, Volvo, Crest, and Federal Express. The fact that you and many millions of others will think "delivers," "safety," "cavities," and "overnight," Ries says, shows that "the most powerful concept in business today is owning a word in the prospect's mind." Word ownership is unlikely for a company that lacks focus; "and focus consistently outperforms diversification." Evidence of the ills of diversification is found in General Motors as an automotive supermarket and American Express as a financial supermarket, Ries asserts. The opposite approach was taken by Howard Schultz, who had the audacity to open Starbucks, "a coffee shop that specialized in, of all things, coffee." Similarly,

"Fred Smith narrowed the [FedEx] focus to small packages, overnight."[10]

NEW BUSINESSES SHOULD ALWAYS BE ON YOUR HORIZON[8]

In *The Alchemy of Growth*, an extensive study of how companies achieve sustained success, McKinsey & Company consultants Stephen Coley, Mehrdad Baghai, and David White found that enduring firms have a continuous pipeline of new businesses that represent new sources of profit: "They can innovate in their core businesses and build new ones at the same time." They do so by constantly keeping endeavors moving through three distinct stages, or "horizons":

◆ *Horizon 1:* encompasses the businesses that are at the heart of an organization – those that customers and stock analysts most readily identify with the corporate name and that usually account for the lion's share of profits and cash flow.

◆ *Horizon 2:* comprises businesses on the rise – fast-moving, entrepreneurial ventures in which a concept is taking root or growth is accelerating.

◆ *Horizon 3:* contains the seeds of tomorrow's businesses – options on future opportunities. Although embryonic, these options are more than ideas; they are real activities and investments.

But haven't both Starbucks and FedEx diversified? Yes – as has Cisco – but each has done so while staying within the realm of its core customers and competencies. The importance of growing in this way, rather than in an unfocused way, is highlighted in *The Alchemy of Growth*, by McKinsey & Company consultants Stephen Coley, Mehrdad Baghai, and David White. They assert that, "Successful companies can and must outlive their individual businesses. They must grow new businesses. That's what leads to sustained, profitable growth."[11]

And it happens with constant attention to focus. "When we look at successful growth companies," the McKinsey authors write, "we see focus, but that doesn't mean on one single kind of business. . . . What they do focus on are the things they do best: their capabilities."

Yes, that means smart companies will pass up seemingly attractive opportunities outside their core capabilities. Sacrifice, Ries claims, is part and parcel of focus. "It may necessarily involve giving up some portion of the market, some versions of the product, or some distribution channel." It may also involve giving up "a short-term boost in revenues," he adds, "but you become stronger over the long term when you reduce the scope of your operations. You can't stand for something if you chase after everything."[12]

FOR PEAK INNOVATION, GO HORIZONTAL

If you think a vertical organization structure works better today than a horizontal one, writes *Business Week*'s John Byrne, think about a swarm of bees: "You might assume a leaderless group of creatures would be ineffectual. Not at all. While one bee is merely a nuisance, a swarm is deadly. 'You only have to look at biological systems to see that there are no big hierarchical stacks,' says Peter Cochrane, head of research at BT Labs. 'Everything is low and flat, very adaptable and very cruel.'

"The Internet allows companies to be more like beehives,"

Byrne continues, "because information can be shared horizontally rather than funneled up to the CEO's office and back down again. . . . The beauty of such leveling is that decisions can be made instantly by the people best equipped to make them. Might that produce corporate chaos? Sure. But that's not necessarily a bad thing. Uniform thinking enforced from the top can cripple an organization."[13]

No such crippling hobbles Cisco, where John Chambers extends the horizontal model beyond the company and throughout its "Internet ecosystem." He grasps the potency of the swarm, saying, "Companies with vertical business models, such as IBM and Honeywell, always get beat by companies with horizontal models. . . . We prefer to follow a horizontal model and work with other players."[14]

And his partners apparently appreciate that stance. Michael R. Rich, president and COO of Cisco partner NetSpeak, credits Cisco with creating:

> . . . the world's greatest horizontal infrastructure – gateways, routers, networking products. . . . The other players, Nortel and Lucent, are far more vertically integrated. So in trying to provide value-added services in those environments, in many cases you actually wind up competing with home-grown or vendor-specific applications, and that makes it harder to sell.[15]

Partners such as NetSpeak provide one sort of horizontal link for Cisco; another is provided by acquisitions. "You've got to be able to provide that horizontal capability in your product line," Chambers explains, "either through your own R&D or through acquisitions."[16]

There's more merit to adding horizontal capabilities via acquisition than just grabbing talent and extending the product line. The horizontal model as pursued by Cisco – in which new technologies are developed in risky startups that are eventually bought by Cisco – also has the advantage of keeping a highly entrepreneurial venture separate from mature, established business units.

"Companies with vertical business models, such as IBM and Honeywell, always get beat by companies with horizontal models."

The importance of such a structure is illustrated by Harvard Business School professor Clayton M. Christensen in *The Innovator's Dilemma: When New Technologies Cause Great Firms to Fail.* He convincingly demonstrates that highly successful, well-managed companies have time and again fallen victim to their own best-intentioned decisions *not* to allocate sufficient resources to the development of "disruptive" technologies. They do this, odd as it may seem, because they are so responsive to customers. For example, established electronic appliance manufacturers wouldn't put poorly performing early transistors into their radios; so "cheap" transistor radios were first developed and brought out by then-obscure Sony of Japan.[17]

Christensen's recommended solution to the innovator's dilemma, reduced to its essence, is for established firms to separate their entrepreneurial endeavors as much as possible from mature units – structurally, financially, and geographically. IBM did it right when it set up a separate, distant organization to develop the company's first personal computers. That's necessary, Christensen concludes, because "the processes that successful, well-managed companies have developed to allocate resources among proposed investments are *incapable* of funneling resources into programs that current customers explicitly don't want and whose profit margins seem unattractive. So it appears that current leaders can only develop disruptive technologies outside their existing corporate structure."

Cisco's top team – intentionally or not – is heeding Christensen's advice by allowing disruptive innovation to occur independently, as it must, in high-risk, high-energy startups.

LEVERAGE YOUR WINNERS TO PRODUCE MORE WINS

In its proprietary Internetwork Operating System (IOS) software, Cisco possesses the key to dominating markets for a range of Internet products and services – markets in which it might otherwise rank only as an also-ran. The magic of IOS, according to *PC Week*, was unintended and unrecognized when it was developed by Cisco's founders "because no other software was available to run on the router they invented." But IOS became "a de facto industry standard for networking." Result: "Customers are effectively locked into Cisco's architecture. . . . Many customers, fearing incompatibility issues, won't even consider rival products."[19]

Cisco officials frequently disclaim any such IOS power, clearly wishing to discourage anyone (particularly US Department of Justice officials) from thinking "IOS is to Cisco as Windows is to Microsoft." Such protestations are apparently unconvincing to the analyst who calls IOS "the most leveraged piece of software in the industry next to Windows."

The leverage he refers to is Cisco's use of IOS as what *PC Week* calls "a launching pad for Cisco to enter new markets. It's a key part of Cisco's growth strategy: Buy smaller companies developing innovative products, take their technology and build it into IOS, with which most network administrators are already familiar."

Even Cisco executives have to acknowledge that IOS gives the company a big boost into new markets. "IOS' overriding benefit is that it provides a common set of services and has a common look and feel [across a lot of Cisco products]," ac-

---

CONVERGENCE COMBATANTS: TALE OF THE TAPE[18]

Until recently, the transmission of data signals was a line of business unto itself, as was transmission of voice and video communications. Now, those formerly discrete offerings are converging – a single "pipe" will increasingly carry all three types of signals simultaneously. While companies such as Alcatel, Ericsson, Siemens, 3Com, and a host of ambitious start-ups figure prominently in the battle to control certain market segments, the head-to-head-to-head combatants in virtually all venues are Cisco, Lucent, and Nortel. Here's a tale-of-the-tape glimpse of each:

Cisco Systems

Background: A routers-only manufacturer in its early years that caught the Internet wave to become king of data transmission networking. Now barging aggressively into the Lucent/Nortel dominated domain of voice telecommunications equipment and the converged transmission of data, video, and voice.

Annual revenues: $12 billion   *Employees:* 21,000

Strengths: King of the hill in networking gear. Possessor of proprietary IOS (Internetwork Operating System) software that often leaves buyers with no practical choice but Cisco. Plus, its record of stock appreciation makes Cisco options an extremely valuable sort of currency the company uses to buy its way into new markets and capabilities.

Weaknesses: No history in the "old world" market of telephone gear, where the Baby Bells and other telecommunications behemoths have long-standing relationships and deep trust in Lucent and Nortel.

Key acquisition: Cerent Corp., a developer of high-speed fiber-optic equipment, helped Cisco plug a perceived gap in its product line – devices called ATM (asynchronous transfer mode) switches – and significantly shrink Nortel's advantage in optical systems, which look to be the medium of choice for converged signal transmission.

Strategy: Push new world IP (Internet protocol) technologies relentlessly, convincing current and prospective customers to break completely – rather than incrementally – with the past, i.e. Lucent and Nortel.

Lucent Technologies Inc.

Background: Formed by the spin-off by AT&T of two old Bell System units: the workhorse telephone equipment manufacturer, Western Electric, and the storied R&D arm, Bell Labs.

Annual revenues: $33 billion   *Employees:* 142,000

Strengths: Long-time leader in voice switches and widely considered tops among major telecom players in fiber optics. A world-renowned innovator – Bell Labs produces an average 3.5 patents daily.

Weaknesses: Still burdened with some of the telephone system products and cultural remnants of its smug, plodding "Ma Bell" days. Viewed by some as too wedded to use of ATM technology, whose days are numbered by eventual global adoption of IP products and services.

Key acquisition: Ascend Communications, in June 1999, plugged a gap in offerings to big carriers and signaled Cisco that Lucent is ready to rumble.

Strategy: Keep long-term customers who value Lucent's unsurpassed reliability, while relying on fiber optics to chip away at Cisco's base in the formerly all-data market.

Nortel Networks Corp.

Background: Grew up as Northern Electric, a telephone equipment manufacturer that supplied and was largely owned by Bell Canada (whose parent company today, BCE, owns 40% of Nortel).

Annual revenues: $18 billion *Employees:* 76,000

Strengths: Straddles yesterday and tomorrow as leading supplier in the traditional circuit-telephony world and in converged optical systems. Regarded as tops when it comes to implementation and expertise.

Weaknesses: Burdened with large share of revenues provided by traditional telephone equipment – a slow-growing market segment and one that provides relatively slim gross margins. Viewed by some as weak in marketing.

Key acquisition: Internet and data equipment maker Bay Networks, in August 1998, struck at Cisco's enterprise market.

Strategy: Nudge customers along a path of steady migration to new world technologies, with "hybrid" Nortel gear that mixes old telephone hardware with new Internet features. De-emphasize equipment in favor of more profitable software and services.

cording to Cisco enterprise marketing VP Peter Alexander. He demurely adds, "There are times when that adds value and times when it doesn't."

Bill Gatesian excessive modesty aside, Cisco officials are likely hoping that IOS can be extended into converged voice- and data-networking products. At least one Silicon Valley venture capitalist would appear to like the company's chances: "Having proprietary control over an architecture in the heart of a tornado market represents the acme of gorilla power . . . and Cisco has it."[20]

KEEP CHANGING TO KEEP COMPETING

With IOS, "Customers are effectively locked into Cisco's architecture. . . . Many customers, fearing incompatibility issues, won't even consider rival products." – PC Week

"Cisco was founded on the strength of a single product, but its growth has been driven by its ability to remain on the leading edge of the ever-expanding and changing vision of exactly what end-to-end networking means." In this single sentence, *Future Focus* authors Al Ries and Theodore B. Kinni divulge – probably as concisely as anyone inside or outside Cisco ever has – the secret of Cisco's unequaled growth.[21]

That secret was also uncovered in a study by McKinsey & Company consultants Stephen Coley, Mehrdad Baghai, and David White. In their book *The Alchemy of Growth*, they assert that, "Successful companies can and must outlive their individual businesses. They must grow new businesses. That's what leads to sustained, profitable growth."[22]

The consultants comment on Cisco's preferred path to sustained growth, acquisitions, noting that the key consideration is "whether the two companies together will grow more quickly than they would have separately. That would be the case if the two companies find ways to benefit from the capabilities that each brings to the deal. For example, perhaps one oil company is good at finding oil and the other is better at extracting it. . . . But if cost savings are all you get from a merger, then you're leaving value on the table." Chambers has repeatedly said cost savings is not a top factor in Cisco's consideration of any potential acquisition.

> "Having proprietary control over an architecture in the heart of a tornado market represents the acme of gorilla power . . . and Cisco has it." – A Silicon Valley venture capitalist

Cisco's headline-grabbing acquisition of Cerent Corp. in 1999 is typical of deals in which Cisco is clearly aiming to benefit over time from mutually reinforcing strengths. Cerent's technology provides Cisco with the ideal link between Cisco's existing Internet gear and the emerging light-speed transmission of converged data, voice, and video via fiber optics. Chambers termed the Cerent deal a "breakaway moment" for Cisco; *Business Week* noted, "Analysts think he's on to something."[23]

More important, Cisco's customers apparently think Chambers is on to something. A rapid-fire series of strategic moves by Cisco in mid-1999 prompted *Information Week* to observe that Cisco "apparently wants to expand its reach across the entire world of communications," with new offerings that "would mean enterprise voice, data, and other kinds of traffic would be handled by a common infrastructure of Cisco switches and routers, regardless of whether it travels over a LAN or WAN, a private or public network." That prospect looks good to a Polaroid Corp. network manager and Cisco customer, who says, "We're looking to Cisco to provide a high level of integration between its enterprise and service-provider products. Using common platforms that work together would make life easier for me."[24]

"[Cisco's] growth has been driven by its ability to remain on the leading edge of the ever-expanding and changing vision of exactly what end-to-end networking means." – *Future Focus*, by Al Ries and Theodore B. Kinni

Cisco's continual transitioning into new lines of business that are responsive to needs of Polaroid and other customers adhere to the recommendations of Adrian J. Slywotzky, a partner in Mercer Management Consulting and coauthor of *The Profit Zone: How Strategic Business Design Will Lead You to Tomorrow's Profits*. He claims companies have to adjust to today's "customer-centric" world, in which buyers have unprecedented access to information and suppliers almost anywhere on the planet, and have access to products and services that exactly meet their needs. What's more, Slywotzky adds, customers' needs and priorities are continually changing, which means suppliers must continually change to respond to customers' shifts. "Yesterday's profit zone – the place where customers allowed you to make a profit – is today's no-profit zone."

Slywotzky says that many companies adopt and later drop many different "profit models" in their successful quests to stay in the profit zone (see sidebar). No model is right all the time or necessarily right for any other company. Instead, "each model has proven to be the right one at the right time for the company that adopted it. That comes from customer-centric thinking – and from recognizing that it will be the right model only until the profit zone shifts again."[25]

SERVE YOUR CORE CUSTOMERS FROM START TO END-TO-END

When it comes to data networking, Cisco is top-of-mind for a range of customers that have widely divergent needs. The company is responsive to all of them, which reinforces its top-of-mind positioning in a virtuous cycle that generates current and future profitability. Make it happen for your firm, too, with these critical measures:

◆ *Be everything your customers need.* A healthy company is a growing company; one that's not growing is not long for this world. Why? Because what your customers want is continually changing. If you're static, you can't meet their emerging needs.

◆ *. . . and no more than your customers need.* By deciding what your business is, you implicitly decide what it is not. It's important to go where customers take you, provided you stick with your core capabilities. When customers go elsewhere, meet their needs through your horizontal business model.

◆ *For peak innovation, go horizontal.* The horizontal business model reaches out through a network of customers, suppliers, and partners to work in the best interests of all participants. No company has had more success with the model than Cisco, which has escaped many of the ills of bigness by working so effectively with others.

◆ *Leverage your winners to produce more wins.* Success breeds success in business as in other aspects of life. Winning products and services open doors for other products and services, in a dynamic that can pervade end-to-end offerings.

◆ *Keep changing to keep competing.* To succeed over the long term, continually reassess and alter your mix of products and services to respond to customer needs. Because any enduring company is actually a

---

FOLLOW CUSTOMERS TO THE END-TO-END OF THE EARTH[26]

For sustained success over time, a company must adopt "customer-centric" thinking, according to consultant Adrian J. Slywotzky of Mercer Management Consulting. That means you listen continually to customers, perceive their ever-changing wants, and follow them to new "profit zones" where they'll "allow you to make a profit." Here's how a few standout companies have successfully done it:

◆ *Coca-Cola* – foresaw that it could not continue to succeed by remaining primarily a syrup maker and advertiser, so it bought out its bottlers.

◆ *Disney* – had to shift from being solely a content creator and move into content distribution. When value later migrated to retailing the products for which Disney had previously only gotten licensing fees, the company moved into retailing. One result was that the company made $400 million from *The Lion King* at the movie box office, but $1.8 billion from tied-in ancillary merchandising.

◆ *Intel* – has stayed in the profit zone, Slywotzky says, "for the most part by maintaining a two-year lead on its competitors, thus getting profits from new products before unit prices come way down."

Each of these companies has gone where it had to when it had to, Slywotzky observes, as a result of customer-centric thinking. And each is prepared to move again when customers once more shift the profit zone.

succession of businesses, conducted over time by an ongoing corporate entity. The only constant is change.

NOTES

1. Schwartz, Nelson D., and Creswell, Julie, "10 Stocks to Grow With," *Fortune*, 16 August 1999.

2. Murray, Maryanne, et al., "Digital 50," *Time Digital*, 4 October 1999.

3. DiCarlo, Lisa, "King of the Jungle: Cisco's Grip on the Networking Market Keeps Prices High, Rivals Out," *PC Week*, 22 February 1999.

4. Daly, James, "The Art of the Deal," *Business 2.0*, October 1999.

5. Schwartz, Nelson D., and Creswell, Julie, "10 Stocks to Grow With," *Fortune*, 16 August 1999.

6. Riggs, Brian, and Wallace, Bob, "Cisco in Charge – Networking Vendor Flexes its Enterprise Muscle," *InformationWeek*, 6 September 1999.

7. Uncredited, "How Big Companies Grow," *Harvard Management Update*, May 1999.

8. Coley, Stephen, Baghai, Mehrdad, and White, David, *The Alchemy of Growth*, Perseus, Cambridge, Massachusetts, 1999.

9. Ries, Al, and Kinni, Theodore B., *Future Focus*, Capstone, Oxford, 2000.

10. Author interview.

11. Coley, Stephen, Baghai, Mehrdad, and White, David, *The Alchemy of Growth*, Perseus, Cambridge, Massachusetts, 1999.

12. Author interview.

13. Byrne, John A., "21 Ideas for the 21st Century: The Global Corporation Becomes the Leaderless Corporation," *Business Week*, 30 August 1999.

14. Janah, Monua, "Computer-Networking Firms Seek to Boost Sales," *San Jose Mercury News*, 11 August 1999.

15. Uncredited, "Breaking Out of the In Pack," *Intelligent Network News*, 13 October 1999.

16. Daly, James, "The Art of the Deal," *Business 2.0*, October 1999.

17. Presentation at International Strategic Leadership Forum, Washington, DC, April 1997.

18. Compiled from numerous reports.

19. DiCarlo, Lisa, "King of the Jungle: Cisco's Grip on the Networking Market Keeps Prices High, Rivals Out," *PC Week*, 22 February 1999.

20. DiCarlo, Lisa, "King of the Jungle: Cisco's Grip on the Networking Market Keeps Prices High, Rivals Out," *PC Week*, 22 February 1999.

21. Ries, Al, and Kinni, Theodore B., *Future Focus*, Capstone, Oxford, 2000.

22. Coley, Stephen, Baghai, Mehrdad, and White, David, *The Alchemy of Growth*, Perseus, Cambridge, Massachusetts, 1999.

23. Reinhardt, Andy, "The Man Who Hones Cisco's Cutting Edge," *Business Week*, 13 September 1999.

24. Riggs, Brian, and Wallace, Bob, "Cisco in Charge – Networking Vendor Flexes its Enterprise Muscle," *InformationWeek*, 6 September 1999.

25. Presentation at International Strategic Leadership Forum, New York, April 1998.

26. Presentation at International Strategic Leadership Forum, New York, April 1998.

Seven

LOOK TO LEAD IN EVERY LINE OF BUSINESS

IN THIS CHAPTER

How has Cisco so successfully come to dominate its 20 key markets less than 15 years after its sole product was assembled on the founders' living room floor? And what are the advantages – beyond bragging rights – of being top dog in a statistical measure that says nothing about profitability? This chapter reveals the Cisco market-share secrets that can boost your firm's bottom-line performance.

John Chambers unabashedly names General Electric CEO Jack Welch as one of his personal management heroes,[1] and perhaps most reflects Welch in his dedication to seeing his company achieve a number 1 or 2 market share in every line of business.

For Chambers – as for Welch – the objective has been achieved across the board. Cisco's annual report says the company "holds the number one market share position in 16 of the 20 key markets in which we compete. We hold the number two position in the remaining four areas."

WHY MARKET SHARE STILL MATTERS[2]

"As a measure of corporate success, market share has slipped out of fashion," observes Stuart Crainer, in his book *Business the Jack Welch Way*. But Welch "remains a fan." Why? Crainer lists four reasons:

◆ Market share is an easily understood rallying point. "Everyone . . . can understand what market share means."

◆ It gives businesses "clear criteria for success or failure. They know where they stand."

◆ It's not an obsession, or even an overriding philosophy – "just a convenient rationale." Welch uses market share and then moves on.

◆ GE tends to be in businesses where market share matters. So Welch, by targeting the number one or two share slot in every line of business, is helping GE create value.

GIVE YOURSELF A FIGHTING CHANCE

John Chambers and Jack Welch, among other superb CEOs, are hardly risk-averse. But neither do they take foolish chances. They boldly charge into hotly competitive markets – as Chambers has done in entering the fray for share in converged voice and data transmission – but do so selectively. Where they don't have a fighting chance of grabbing a top share spot, they leave it to others to duke it out. "We never enter a market where we don't think we can become number one or two," the Cisco chief says.[3]

"We never enter a market where we don't think we can become number one or two."

Within the IT industry, Chambers says, "We will never be a service provider, a systems integrator, or have a large role in consulting. We will not be in a market where we don't bring an expertise or an advantage, and a minimum of 25 percent market share, with 40 percent plus being our goal."[4]

With such remarks, Chambers reflects – consciously or not – the thinking of his hero Jack Welch, who says that in choosing GE's markets, "We've tried to play to our strengths, like aircraft engines, like materials."

"We will not be in a market where we don't bring an expertise or an advantage, and a minimum of 25 percent market share, with 40 percent plus being our goal."

Welch recalls that he launched GE's effort to achieve a top share ranking in each of the company's markets by asking a question suggested by management guru Peter F. Drucker: "If you weren't already in this business, would you enter it now?" With his top team, Welch subjected every one of GE's diverse, far-flung units to the Drucker test, hanging on to the business only if it:

◆ is heavily technology-related,

◆ is capital intensive, and

◆ doesn't operate on short cycle times.[5]

Those criteria were selected, logically enough, because they represented GE's core strengths. "We're the fastest elephant at the dance," Welch says, "but we are still an elephant." So GE's housewares division got the boot because it required little money and turned on fast cycles. The semiconductor unit, too, was dropped. It was fine on the technology and capital requirements, but flunked the cycle-time test.[6] And so GE's slimming proceeded, until all of the firm's retained units were "involved in only those businesses that were, or could become, either number one or number two in their global markets."[7]

When the dust finally settled from Welch's initial top-spot review process, GE had shed $10 billion worth of non-core businesses. Profitable and promising units were among those to get the heave-ho. Why? Welch says GE's top team insisted on having a realistic shot at a top share ranking "based on our observation that when a number-one market-share business entered a down cycle and 'sneezed,' number four or five often caught galloping pneumonia." As part of the same process, Welch recalls, "we made $19 billion of acquisitions, to strengthen the world-leading businesses we wanted to take with us into the nineties."[8]

GE's selectivity in market participation, like Cisco's, reflects the CEO's recognition that even the best-run companies can't be all things to all people. Market leaders can't be unequaled in everything, so they shoot for being unequaled in a particular way. Consultants Michael Treacy and Fred Wiersma call this self-imposed restraint the "unique value discipline" in their 1994 book, *The Discipline of Market Leaders.* They define three value disciplines:

◆ *Operational excellence* – focuses not so much on product or service innovation or on cultivating deep customer relationships as on providing "middle-of-the-market products at the best price with the least inconvenience. . . . Wal-Mart epitomizes this kind of company."

◆ *Product leadership* – practitioners "concentrate on offering products that push performance boundaries." They provide "the best product, period, [and] continue to innovate year after year." Examples: Intel and Nike.

◆ *Customer intimacy* – adherents "focus on delivering not what the market wants but what specific customers want. . . . Airborne Express practices customer intimacy with a vengeance, achieving success . . . by consistently going the extra mile for its selectively chosen customers."

Market leaders "don't shine in every way," Treacy and Wiersma write. Instead, they "are thriving because they shine in a way their customers care most about. They have honed at least one component of value to a level of excellence that puts all competitors to shame."[9]

CHAMBERS ON HOW TO BE NO. 1 [10]

Which companies will be the big winners in the new economy? John Chambers says the firms that rise to the top will:

♦ **Structure horizontally.** "Horizontal companies will win. They always have."

♦ **Adopt open standards.** "Proprietary standards are gone. . . . PBXs are dead."

♦ **Attract and keep talent.** "A handful of really bright engineers will outproduce 1,000 engineers."

♦ **Move fast.** "If you can't be fast, you're going to get left behind."

♦ **Focus on customers.** Any company and any industry that doesn't have its finger on the customer will get left behind."

♦ **Use Internet technology.** Without it, "you can't . . . move with the speed to take on the large competitors, or the capability to create the profits."

BE – OR BUY – A FIRST MOVER

Bill Gates, at one time, was roundly criticized from all quarters – by customers, competitors, analysts, and others – for being first-to-market with products that had more bugs than the woods surrounding the Microsoft chief's lakeside home.

No more. Today, Gates is lauded for having understood, before just about anyone else, the value of so-called "first-mover advantage." A first mover pushes to get products to market as fast as possible, because mind share translates into market share. In his book about Microsoft, *I Sing the Body Electronic*, Fred Moody reports, "The value of being first rather than best . . . was too much a part of the Microsoft culture ever to be questioned."[11]

John Chambers appears to have adopted and modified the speed-freak principle: Cisco is first to market, but often with substantially bug-free products. "Time to market is key in this industry," he says. "If you don't make the window, you never become one or two. IBM used to believe they could be number six through fifteen in the market and become number one. As you know, that did not happen, and it wouldn't happen in this industry either."[12]

> "Time to market is key in this industry. If you don't make the window, you never become one or two."

Gaining first-mover advantage, according to London's *Financial Times*, is Chambers' "driving force behind both internal product development and acquisitions."[13] The CEO's remarks indicate the *FT* is right on the money. For example, he's said,

> I've always believed that a good indication of how well your R&D group is functioning is how well you develop products internally. . . . At the same time, we have a real firm rule: If we're not in the first five to market for an important technology, we partner with one of the first five or we acquire one of the first five. And I don't give our engineers a choice on that.[14]

Dozens of Cisco alliances and acquisitions prove Chambers true to his word – none more so than the company's $6.9 billion buy of Cerent Corp., a company that had never shown a profit, but possessed an optical transmission technology that Cisco couldn't hope to soon buy elsewhere or replicate internally. After the initial shock of the mega-purchase had worn off, the consensus among analysts was that Cisco would get its money's worth from Cerent. "[That's] a lot of money for a company without much revenue," says one. "But relative to what Cisco is getting out of the deal, I don't think it's a bad move."[15]

First-mover advantage may well be worth Cerent's price and more, based on its importance to Boston Consulting Group VPs Philip Evans and Thomas S. Wurster. In their book *Blown to Bits: How the New Economics of Information Transforms Strategy*, they claim, "The only sure loser is the 'fast follower.' Fast followers are *always* too late. It is better to be too early five times than to be too late once."[16]

> "The only sure loser is the 'fast follower.' Fast followers are *always* too late. It is better to be too early five times than to be too late once." – *Blown to Bits*, by Philip Evans and Thomas S. Wurster

Today, it's usually a good move to be a first mover, according to consultant David H. Jones, because of the accelerating pace of change. "As recently as the early 1980s," he says, "IBM was a johnny-come-lately to the personal computer wars – yet they were able to rise quickly to market leadership. But today change is so rapid and continuous that there's considerable doubt as to whether Apple, for example, will ever recapture its former market share."

A key difference between then and now, Jones contends, is the "cycle time" of knowledge. "It's become so short that, by the time a second-tier organization acquires the knowledge that previously boosted its world-class competitor, that competitor has itself acquired the next generation of knowledge. Unless the leader loses its way, the second-tier player can't catch up."[17]

CISCO'S MARKET SHARES IN KEY CHANNELS[18]

◆ *Internet service providers* – About 80 percent of all Internet routers in use are Cisco products, but the company is waging a two-front war against aggressive startups, such as Juniper Networks, and established giants, such as Lucent, Nortel, and 3Com. *Cisco's share:* 33 percent of the $9 billion market.

◆ *Telephone companies* – Cisco has little history and less clout among the "old world" telcos, which are rapidly migrating into the new world as transmission of data and voice converge. *Cisco's share:* Less than 1 percent of the $225 billion market.

◆ *Enterprises* – Cisco gets more than half of its $12 billion-plus revenue from the big companies that compose this market, and is likely to boost that portion owing to a 1999 deal with IBM. *Cisco's share:* 40 percent of the $16 billion market.

◆ *Small and medium businesses* – With its arm-lock grip on the enterprise market, Cisco has recently focused more on firms in this sector. *Cisco's share:* 18 percent of the $14 billion market.

◆ *Consumers* – The market for networking gear in homes is projected to soar to $4 billion in 2002, and Cisco is maneuvering to grab as much of that revenue as possible. Chief rivals here are 3Com and Intel. *Cisco's share:* 10 percent of the under-$250 million market.

DON'T FORGET OLD-FASHIONED SALESMANSHIP

Cisco has soared to fame and fortune with website sales as its main rocket. So you may be surprised to learn that the company, with only some 20,000 total employees – fields a

---

WITH ENEMIES LIKE THESE, WHO NEEDS FRIENDS?[19]

John Chambers claims that part of the credit for Cisco's across-the-board market-share leadership goes to his company's worthy competitors – not for being pushovers, but scrappers. He says he learned:

> . . . the very hard way at IBM and Wang what happens when you don't have competition. . . . You get soft, and a new company comes in and displaces you. So not only is it ethically wrong to eliminate your competition, it's just bad business judgment. I will have more market share [in] five years because I have good competitors now, than I will if I don't have any.

6,000-person strong sales force.[20] Intel Chairman Andy Grove calls Cisco's sales operation "the little-told advantage of Cisco . . . a key element of their success."[21]

Key enough to win third place in "America's Best Sales Forces" rankings for 1999 by *Sales & Marketing Management* magazine (only Enron and Dell Computer finished higher). *S&MM* was particularly impressed with Cisco's "skill at building a winning team of direct salespeople and channel partners."[22]

That Cisco's sales force shines owes in no small measure to John Chambers' background in sales at IBM. *The Wall Street Journal* was moved to remark that, when it comes to sales, Cisco "still lives and dies by the shoe leather of old-fashioned salesmanship" that "doesn't resemble Amazon.com so much as IBM in its heyday in the '70s." The *Journal* article paints a picture of Cisco sales that is composed equally of elements from the "Old Economy" – a top sales rep "fits the mold of the backslapping, joke-cracking salesman" – and the New – prospective customers with Kodak are plied with an opportunity to associate with "the company that is making the World Wide Web come alive."[23]

But it is Cisco's approach to selling small and medium-size businesses, rather than large ones, that wins praise from *S&MM*. The magazine notes that Cisco wisely recognized that its "traditional direct sales model" could never be made to work in a volatile world of tens of thousands small-to-medium firms. "The new model: Account managers work with resellers, some of which already have relationships with small- and medium-size businesses. . . . [Some] resellers find new clients without ever involving a Cisco rep."[24]

A more recent Cisco effort is aimed at getting resellers to place a greater share of orders through the Internet. That further leverages Cisco's sales force – but exposes the company to greater risk of losing direct regular contact with customers. "I prefer the personal contact," a Jacksonville, Florida, reseller says. "The ability to work on the Web is great when there is no complexity. But if I want to make an impression on a customer, I want to have a rep with me."[25]

Cisco is clearly feeling its way – as are most firms – in shaping a sales force that provides an optimum balance between effectiveness and efficiency in the Internet age. The *Journal* article notes that "the Cisco sales force plays down its technology . . . in favor of 'business solutions.'" *S&MM* says its "1999 Best Sales Force companies demonstrate that the winning enterprises are nimble enough – and bold enough – to adapt to change."

Selling solutions and adapting to change are key indicators of sales success in the 21st century, according to an article in *Harvard Management Update*. Experts surveyed for the article "agree that the evolutionary path of sales has recently split forever," such that all products and services are sold in one of two ways – either:

◆ *commoditization* – where competing products and services are virtually identical and, therefore, bought on the "transactional" basis of price alone – increasingly, via the Internet – or

◆ *consultation* – or relationship selling, where buyers need and want assistance in making their purchase decision and have more recently begun to demand ongoing input from sellers, such as help in applying solutions to the buyer's specific circumstances and uses.[26]

Like most companies that provide more than a single product or service, Cisco has many offerings that fit with commoditized sales and many others suited to consultative selling. "How do you choose the most advantageous route?" the *Harvard* article asks. A sales executive suggests you "think of yourself as the buyer" and consider whether you'd like to meet with a sales consultant. "If you know the book you want is Grisham's latest legal thriller, the answer is no – and transactional superstars like Amazon.com have capitalized on that fact. But if you're buying global computer networking for one of the newly merged oil giants, you'd likely welcome the input of a veritable army of consultative sellers."

GUIDANCE ON "BIFURCATED" SALES OF THE INTERNET AGE[27]

Sales experts agree that "an apparently permanent bifurcation [of sales] is channeling every product and service into one of two paths": either commoditization, exemplified by low-price, high-volume, dot-com superstars such as Amazon, or consultation (or relationship) selling, where complicated, multi-component "solutions" can't be bought without the assistance of a seller's sales consultant. Each of the two types of sales is characterized by very different guidelines for success.

In the case of your commoditized products and services:

◆ *Sales people are money pits.* The customer already has all the product information that sales reps used to provide – and more, from comparative performance figures to the factory invoice price. In this environment, the sales rep is seen by the customer as a barrier to the purchase.

◆ *Your patented, reversible, titanium gotwhocky is irrelevant.* With immediate worldwide flow and availability of information and materials, differentiations between competing items have been virtually eliminated – if not in fact, then in the customer's mind.

◆ *You need to perfect the inhuman touch.* Winners in the commoditized world are the sellers – such as Dell Computer and Charles Schwab – that can use emerging technologies to bond with customers.

On the other hand, in the realm of consultative or relationship selling:

◆ *Subtract the sales rep who's no more than a mouthpiece.* Any sales position you support in the consultative world has got to create value for customers to be worthwhile for you. The value creator demonstrates a skill set that would once have seemed more suited to psychiatry than sales; he or she focuses not on persuading, but on understanding the customer.

♦ **Know your customers better than they know themselves.** The consultative seller has to go to the customer with precisely the message the customer wants to hear. Today, schmoozing is losing – where the schmooze is any sales pitch not grounded in solid research.

♦ **Get your technical pros out of their pocket protectors and onto your sales team.** The increasing complexity of many products and services makes it impossible for any one person – sales rep or product-design whiz – to know all they can do for a buyer. What's required is team involvement – sales reps and a fungible mix of folks from purchasing, design, engineering, finance, IT, and other formerly behind-the-scenes areas of the organization.

♦ **Talk is cheap; sellers today have got to be communicators.** You don't get the face time with buyers you once got, so the rapport that sales pros establish must increasingly arise from the written, printed, or electronically transmitted word. That means the people who can demonstrate their sales skills in writing will probably do better than those who can't.

LEVERAGE YOUR LEADERSHIP POSITIONS

Good things come with market leadership. Things that don't directly have anything to do with the quality or effectiveness of your employees, your products, your marketing, or your leaders. Perhaps it's unfair, but it's there nonetheless. To wit:

♦ "Dataquest's Mr Smith says its only natural that most of the new optical networking players will eventually be absorbed by the handful of dominant firms in the industry. Market leaders such as Cisco 'always have the muscle to take out the guys with the new technology,' he says." – *National Post*, 13 September 1999[28]

◆ "'We're forced to use [Cisco] technology to maintain compatibility [with customers] because everyone else is using
Cisco,' said Tony Zies, vice president at Concentric Network Corp. 'The reliance we must have on Cisco ultimately
forces us to pay a premium.'" – *PC Week*, 22 February
1999[29]

◆ "'They did in networking what IBM did in the computer
business,' said Peter Bernstein, president of Infonautics
Consulting. 'They managed to convince people that no one
will lose their job by buying Cisco.'" – *Computer Reseller
News*, 13 September 1999[30]

But perhaps the most valuable benefit of market leadership
that can be gained by a dynamic company such as Cisco is the
winner's confidence it can carry into new markets – where
initial share may be next to nonexistent and prospects for eventual leadership anything but certain. Such is Cisco's current
position in trying to establish itself as a supplier of converged
voice-and-data transmission equipment to major telephone
companies.

It's a risky move that has raised eyebrows among some of the
industry observers who most influence Cisco's financial performance and public perception. Example: Paul Sagawa, a
respected and widely quoted analyst at investment banker San-
ford Bernstein & Co., says,

> I don't think [Cisco's] position in the [telecommunications]
> service provider market is as strong as a lot of people in the in-
> vestment community like to believe. They probably have one
> percent of overall service provider spending of about $168 bil-
> lion. Also, they tend to overstate the importance of what they
> call new-world technologies.[31]

Why should Cisco – or your company – risk pervasive dominance of every one of its current markets to enter a market
where it starts with a mere toehold? John Chambers knows: "I
believe you have to change your company almost every
two years. Not just because you feel the need, but
to catch the market in transition. That's how
you gain market share."[32] And – as business
history proves – how you lose it, even if
your company has been wildly successful
thus far in all of its markets. "I think it's
still up for grabs who [the winners] are
going to be, including whether or not
we make it," Chambers says. "Anybody
who thinks they've got a lock on this
future doesn't understand the market
very well."[33]

> "I
> believe you
> have to change
> your company
> almost every two
> years. Not just
> because you feel the
> need, but to catch
> the market in
> transition. That's
> how you gain
> market
> share."

Chambers could almost have been reading
the words of another corporate leader with a
considerable record of dominating markets. In
The Road Ahead, Bill Gates writes, "We have to earn
our leadership position every day. If we stop innovating
or stop adjusting our plans, or if we miss the next big turn in
the industry's road, we'll lose out." Later, Gates is more blunt:
"Death can come swiftly to a market leader."[34]

Ironically, in understanding that past market leadership is no
guarantee of future market performance, perceptive leaders
such as Chambers and Gates probably keep their people from
falling into the collective overconfidence that might reverse
their records of achievement. Even the skeptical analyst Sagawa indicates he knows that Chambers' doubt about Cisco's
future is ultimately healthy: "Cisco has a lot of good people,

and they will find a way to grow their share of service-provider sales."[35]

STEPS TO STAYING ON TOP[36]

In *Market Ownership: The Art & Science of Becoming #1*, William A. Sherden contends that attaining market leadership is not without peril; business history offers many instances of corporate management "succumbing to its own success." His ideas for sustaining market ownership:

◆ *Avoid complacency.* Sherden quotes Home Depot CEO Bernard Marcus: "When we start getting cookie-cutter stores that stay the same year after year, that's when we have to worry about our downfall."

◆ *Set stretch objectives.* Achieved goals should be followed by "new goals that require a quantum leap in value," Sherden writes. Xerox recovered from an almost fatal competitive onslaught by setting new quality improvement goals, achieving them, and becoming "one of the few American companies to regain a market share previously lost to Japanese companies."

◆ *Create a change-tolerant organization.* Because a company's operating environment is always changing, so must the company, Sherden argues – either by choice or by change forced upon it.

◆ *Block the competition.* "Continually restructure your business in small increments to avoid the trauma that results from a major restructuring."

LOOK TO LEAD IN EVERY LINE OF BUSINESS

Dig beneath the surface of market dominance and you find it's not built on magic, but on smart management. Cisco gets to the top of the heap by adhering to these key guidelines:

◆ *Give yourself a fighting chance.* John Chambers – like General Electric's Jack Welch – isn't going to take Cisco where it shouldn't go. Sticking to core competencies means sticking with what you know, leading from strength. It's the surest way to the top.

◆ *Be – or buy – a first mover.* Cisco doesn't pretend to be the networker that's always on the scene firstest with the mostest. When you're not among the first with a new technology, you'll only catch up by acquiring one of the outfits that is.

◆ *Don't forget old-fashioned salesmanship.* Cisco is so integrally associated with new-world technologies that it's easy to forget about the CEO's sales background – and his understanding that sales will probably always call for a well-timed personal touch. Don't neglect this still-essential skill in our wired world.

◆ *Leverage your leadership positions.* More than revenues flow from market leadership – it also involves an aura that you can leverage in other ways to achieve dominance in still more markets.

NOTES

1. Reinhardt, Andy, "The Man Who Hones Cisco's Cutting Edge," *Business Week*, 13 September 1999.

2. Crainer, Stuart, *Business the Jack Welch Way*, Capstone, Oxford, 1999.

3. Taylor, Paul, "A Fast Mover in the Network Race," *Financial Times*, 7 October 1998.

4. Medford, Cassimir, "Unleashing the Internet Economy," *VAR-Business*, 16 November 1998.

5. Neff, Thomas J., and Citrin, James M., *Lessons From the Top: The Search for America's Best Business Leaders*, Currency-Doubleday, New York, 1999.

6. Neff, Thomas J., and Citrin, James M., *Lessons From the Top: The Search for America's Best Business Leaders*, Currency-Doubleday, New York, 1999.

7. Welch, John F., Jr., "Big Is Beautiful," *Executive Excellence*, October 1996.

8. Welch, John F., Jr., "Big Is Beautiful," *Executive Excellence*, October 1996.

9. Treacy, Michael, and Wiersma, Fred, *The Discipline of Market Leaders*, Addison-Wesley, Cambridge, Massachusetts, 1994.

10. Daly, James, "The Art of the Deal," *Business 2.0*, October 1999.

11. Moody, Fred, *I Sing the Body Electronic*, Penguin, New York, 1995.

12. Caron, Jeremiah, "Winding Cisco's Clock," *tele.com*, 19 April 1999.

13. Taylor, Paul, "A Fast Mover in the Network Race," *Financial Times*, 7 October 1998.

14. Caron, Jeremiah, "Winding Cisco's Clock," *tele.com*, 19 April 1999.

15. Dunn, Ashley, "Cisco to Broaden Its Scope at a Cost of $7.4 Billion," *Los Angeles Times*, 27 August 1999.

16. Evans, Philip, and Wurster, Thomas S., *Blown to Bits: How the New Economics of Information Transforms Strategy*, Harvard Business School Press, Boston, 2000.

17. Author interview.

18. Cisco corporate Website and Reinhardt, Andy, "Mr. Internet," *Business Week*, 13 September 1999.

19. Clarke, Hilary, "I'd Like to Teach the World to Surf," *Independent*, 22 November 1998.

20. Cisco corporate news release, 9 August 1999.

21. Gomes, Lee, "The New Economy Is Still Being Driven by the Old Hard Sell," *Wall Street Journal*, 13 August 1999.

22. Uncredited, "Here's to the Winners; Top Sales Forces," *Sales & Marketing Management*, 1 July 1999.

23. Gomes, Lee, "The New Economy Is Still Being Driven by the Old Hard Sell," *Wall Street Journal*, 13 August 1999.

24. Uncredited, "Here's to the Winners; Top Sales Forces," *Sales & Marketing Management*, 1 July 1999.

25. Zarley, Craig, and Semilof, Margie, "The Cisco Kid – the Networking Giant Is Winning Friends in the Channel," *Computer Reseller News*, 13 September 1999.

26. Stauffer, David, "Sales Strategies for the Internet Age," *Harvard Management Update*, July 1999.

27. Stauffer, David, "Sales Strategies for the Internet Age," *Harvard Management Update*, July 1999.

28. Avery, Simon, "Bright Lights in Fibre Optics," *National Post*, 13 September 1999.

29. DiCarlo, Lisa, "King of the Jungle: Cisco's Grip on the Networking Market Keeps Prices High, Rivals Out," *PC Week*, 22 February 1999.

30. Zarley, Craig, and Semilof, Margie, "The Cisco Kid – the Networking Giant Is Winning Friends in the Channel," *Computer Reseller News*, 13 September 1999.

31. Janah, Monua, "Computer-Networking Firms Seek to Boost Sales," *San Jose Mercury News*, 11 August 1999.

32. Brandt, Richard L., "President and CEO of Cisco Systems Inc. John Chambers – on the Future of Communications and the Failure of Deregulation," *Upside*, October 1998.

33. Caron, Jeremiah, "Winding Cisco's Clock," *tele.com*, 19 April 1999.

34. Gates, Bill, *The Road Ahead*, Penguin, New York, 1996.

35. Janah, Monua, "Computer-Networking Firms Seek to Boost Sales," *San Jose Mercury News*, 11 August 1999.

36. Sherden, William A., *Market Ownership: The Art & Science of Becoming #1*, Amacom, New York, 1995.

Eight

BUY RIGHT TO GROW LIKE GANGBUSTERS

IN THIS CHAPTER

Cisco's growth strategy is "simple," according to *The New York Times*: "Whatever research and development its engineers cannot create in-house, it buys."[1] Easier said than done, particularly when what Cisco has done is become the reigning world champion of acquisitions, with a well-oiled machine that can at any given time have six buyouts in various stages of assimilation. This chapter looks at how Chambers and his company make their grow-by-buying magic work.

Go figure mergers and acquisitions: while studies indicate that less than half eventually add shareholder value, the total annual value of M&A activity persistently climbs – to more than $2 trillion in 1998, the seventh consecutive yearly gain.[2] Cisco accounts for an outsized share of that total yearly acquisition action. From 1993 through 1999, Cisco snapped up 48 firms, prompting *CFO* magazine to remark, "At the bazaar of high-tech companies, Cisco Systems Inc. is a compulsive shopper."[3]

Compulsive? Perhaps, provided the term doesn't imply hasty, foolish, or spendthrift – for Cisco's purchasing performance is about as far from these characterizations as any company could be. The firm's principal acquisitions architect is John Chambers, justifiably dubbed "one of the savviest deal makers in corporate America" by *Business 2.0.* "Few understand the complexities of assessing, purchasing, and assimilating a new company as well as Chambers," the publication says.[4]

BUY TO KEEP MOVING AT INTERNET SPEED

You're perched on a bridge, staring into the abyss. Your center of gravity seems to be in two places: your head, and thoughts, directed toward the uncertain jump you're about to make; your feet planted on the ledge of the bridge, tethered to it only by a bungee cord. That scene is described by Christopher Meyer, who heads Ernst & Young's Center for Business Innovation, to picture "where the world is today, anchored in the present but looking toward its uncertain future."

Meyer and futurist Stan Davis use the word "blur" to indicate that forces of speed, intangible assets, and connectivity are "creating a whole new economy" in which everything seems blurred by the rapid pace of change. This is not necessarily a distressing state of affairs, they explain in their book *Blur: The Speed of Change in the Connected Economy*. Meyer sees "enormous opportunities for growth and value creation" for those who grasp the concept of blur and anticipate where it's taking us.[5]

John Chambers and his masterful team of acquisitions experts at Cisco seem to have grasped the concept and presciently anticipated its direction in the world of information transmission. Their acquisition schedule, according to Morgan Stanley Dean Witter analyst George J. Kelly, recognizes that "the Internet doubles in traffic every 100 days. There's nothing in the world except bacteria that grows that fast." If your company is to cope successfully, Kelly says, "you've got to think at Internet speed." Cisco does, aiming for about a two-week spread between when a line manager sponsors a purchase to the time it is announced.[6]

Why buy, rather than grow internally? Expert consensus – at least within the realms of IT and the Internet – holds that adequate internal growth is simply not possible. A representative comment was offered by data-communications analyst Christin Flynn of The Yankee Group, when Cisco rival Lucent announced its $24 billion acquisition of data-networking supplier Ascend Communications:

> It would have taken [Lucent] probably another year, maybe more, to finish the development of [their] ATM core switch. In this marketplace, you just don't have that kind of time anymore. The market is changing so quickly. . . . So why don't you just cut

your time to market in half? . . . Buy the product, buy the engineers, and get a faster time to market.[7]

In addition to speed, there is efficiency and smart risk management in Cisco's style of growth through acquisition. In effect, Cisco (and, increasingly, its top competitors) outsources research and development to the startups it eventually acquires, snapping them up, according to *Fortune* magazine, "just as their technologies are ready to go bigtime."[8]

Chambers is hardly reticent in admitting as much, when James Daly of *Business 2.0* asked him whether mergers and acquisitions aren't just another form of outsourced R&D. "They are a requirement, given how rapidly customer expectations change," the CEO said. A company must be ready with products that respond to these changes, "either through your own R&D or through acquisitions." Thus, "our ideal acquisition is a small startup that has a great technology product on the drawing board that is going to come out in 6 to 12 months. We buy the engineers and the next generation product."

"Our ideal acquisition is a small startup that has a great technology product on the drawing board that is going to come out in 6 to 12 months."

Many expert observers, viewing a range of mergers and acquisitions across time and industries, warn that they often bloat a company to the state of ponderousness. Chambers responds to that possibility by saying,

You'll have to form your own opinion about how nimble we are. . . . Successful companies all crash and burn for the same reason or slow down for the same reason; they get too far away from the customers and employees and they lose their ability to move fast. So we are fanatical about staying close to the customers.[9]

A BRIEF REVIEW OF CISCO'S BUYS[10]

From 1993 through 1999, Cisco bought 48 companies. Among the most notable:

◆ *Crescendo Communications*, in 1993, for $89 million – arguably Cisco's most successful deal, significantly shaped the company Cisco is today, became a model for future acquisitions, and by itself now contributes $3 billion to annual revenues.

◆ *Stratacom*, in 1996, for $4.4 billion – a sum Cisco was willing to part with to get into the market for speedy data switches.

◆ *Granite Systems*, in 1996, for $220 million – a company started by Sun Microsystems founder Andreas Bechtolshiem, is one of few deals generally thought not to have worked out very well for Cisco, "because Granite's product wasn't as far along as Cisco had believed," according to *Fortune*.

◆ *Ardent Communications*, in 1997, for $156 million – a maker of integrated voice, video and data equipment to hook up company branches with headquarters – has been a disappointing venture for Cisco in backing and later buying a startup, because "Cisco micromanaged the company too much," according to Cisco business development VP Michelangelo Volpi.

◆ *Netspeed*, in 1998, for $255 million – a key supplier of technology for high-speed Internet access at home, most notable for being acquired as a result of a Cisco customer – US West – suggesting it.

◆ *Summa Four*, in 1998, for $116 million – marked Cisco's entry into the telephone equipment market, where it so far remains a minor player.

♦ *GeoTel Communications*, in April 1999, for $2 billion – got Cisco into the software business big time; GeoTel manages phone networks and call centers.

♦ *Calista*, of Bucks, England, in August 1999, for $56 million – notable in marking Cisco's first purchase of a non-US outfit in more than a year, with corporate assurances that more buys abroad are on the way.

♦ *Cerent Corp.*, in August 1999, for $6.9 billion – is said by some analysts to be the most ever paid for a privately held technology company; but likely worth it in providing equipment that moves voice and Net traffic onto high-speed optical fibers.

♦ *Monterey Networks*, in August 1999, for $500 million – a vendor of optical gear that gives service providers the ability to instantly increase their network capacity; purchase announced the same day as the Cerent deal, completing a one–two mega-punch by Cisco in optics.

♦ *IBM Network Technologies*, in September 1999, for $300 million – although structured as an alliance, included Big Blue's total exit from the network routers and switches market and hand-off to Cisco of networking division "intellectual property" – as one analyst put it, "a graceful way for IBM to get out of the networking business."

MAKE PEOPLE THE PRIMARY PURPOSE

There are many different motives for mergers and acquisitions, "ranging from the questionable to the defensible," writes consultant Karl Albrecht in his book *Corporate Radar*. There are balance-sheet deals, which may be touted as clever, but amount to a sum of the parts that is "still the sum of the parts." There are crown-jewel buys, in which the purpose is to acquire a "prize asset" and strip away the rest of the acquired company.

And there are the always-popular synergy combinations, where "few measure up to the claims."[11]

None of the eight most common merger motives that Albrecht lists touches on the first and foremost consideration underlying any Cisco acquisition: people. "The key to our success is understanding that we are acquiring people, not technology," says Cisco's Don Listwin. "Technology is moving so quickly that the products are dead in 18 months."[12]

Cisco controller Dennis Powell says acquired employees are so important that, "If we're going to lose the people who are important to the success of the target company, we're probably not going to have an interest" in that outfit in the first place. "We're not interested in just bringing in a product."[13]

"If you pay between $500,000 and $3 million per employee, and all you are doing is buying the current research and the current market share, you're making a terrible investment."

Listwin and Powell reflect John Chambers' thinking. "When we acquire a company, we aren't simply acquiring its current products, we're acquiring the next generation of products through its people," he says. "If you pay between $500,000 and $3 million per employee, and all you are doing is buying the current research and the current market share, you're making a terrible investment."[14]

Cisco isn't unique – particularly among always talent-hungry Silicon Valley firms – in putting people first in considering an acquisition. But it may stand above all others in keeping the employees it acquires. "[Cisco's] turnover rate for employees acquired through mergers is a scant 2.1 percent, vs. an industry average of more than 20 percent," *Fortune* reports. "Its first acquisition, Crescendo, . . . is still run by Crescendo's CEO, Mario Mazzola."[15]

Cisco excels at retention from top to bottom. Upper management is heavily peppered with executives from acquired companies, including several startup founders – the sort of people thought by conventional wisdom to be genetically incapable of holding any slot but the top one. Example: chief technical officer Judy Estrin, founder of Bridge Communications, who was with Precept Software when Cisco acquired it in 1999.[16]

As for keeping the rank-and-file folks, Chambers tells of Intel chairman Andy Grove's address to Cisco employees, where he asked the audience for a show of hands by all employees who came to Cisco in acquisitions. "And 30 percent of the people raised their hand," Chambers recounts. "He was very candid and said [Intel] could not have done that."[17]

While Cisco's acquisitions put people first, it's important to note they don't consider people alone. There's got to be more to a buy than staff, as Vermeer Technologies founder Charles H. Ferguson explains in his book *High Stakes, No Prisoners*. He relates that Netscape portrayed its acquisition of a company called Collabra "as successful because most of its engineers remained with Netscape and several executives joined Netscape's top management. But Collabra's product was based on pre-Internet proprietary systems and was incompatible with the Internet. . . . Netscape got a few executives and some good engineers for $100 million."[18] This indicates the merit of Cisco's measures of an acquisition's success: first, employee retention; second, new product development; and finally, return on investment.[19]

THE WHEELS THAT MAKE CISCO'S DEALS[20]

CFO magazine provides this insight on the Cisco organization and approach to acquisitions:

◆ A centralized Business Development Group reports to the chief technology officer and, through her, to John Chambers.

◆ Outside investment bankers aren't used; in their place Cisco relies on its own finance department.

◆ The company will sometimes launch a formal relationship by taking a minority stake in a potential target startup – six such arrangements have proceeded to acquisition.

◆ A "virtual acquisition team" is formed for each prospective acquisition, with members drawn from the unit interested in the target company and dedicated M&A personnel. Finance contributes as many as eight team members, "combing the target's balance sheet and the income statement."

◆ After a deal is completed, a centralized team of 15–25 people stands ready to take on the integration function.

DON'T SWEAT THE PRESENT, BUY THE FUTURE

Cisco stunned the business world in August 1999 when it announced it would acquire high-tech optical systems developer Cerent Corp. for $6.9 billion, an incredibly steep price for a company that had registered only $10 million in sales during its entire corporate history and had never recorded a profit.

"This is unbelievable and unprecedented," said a technology investment banker, whose words were typical of those uttered by participants in every aspect of the IT industry.

Had Cisco's vaunted acquisitions team at last stumbled – bought the Brooklyn Bridge like a country bumpkin on his first trip to the Big Apple? Fat chance – as was recognized in the further comments of just about everyone quoted on the deal, including that investment banker, who said the acquisition "is truly reflective of the *expectations* [emphasis added] for how the Internet infrastructure is going to be forced to evolve to support the demands of e-commerce."[21]

Cisco's Cerent acquisition – like the 40-odd other that preceded it – was all about the future and little about the present. "This new market for Cisco will be a double-digit billion-dollar opportunity," says Cisco CFO Larry Carter, who pegged the value of Cerent's target optical-transport market at $10 billion in 2002. He noted that optical networks are expected to become a fast-growing segment of Internet infrastructure. "With this technology, Cisco can easily accommodate the changes needed in bandwidth traffic. The real issue here is, how do you deal with Internet growth?"[22]

In a broader sense, isn't any merger or acquisition about how you deal with growth – or its absence? Morgan Stanley's Kelly notes that in the blurred world of data networking and telecommunications, "Everything is so strategic and the market opportunities are so great, [immediate returns] are not relevant."[23]

Chambers agrees, saying that in Cisco's buys, "we are not acquiring current market share. We are acquiring futures."[24] On another occasion, he elaborates: "We look at a certain revenue stream that we think we can generate from the acquired company, looking out two to three years. So for our smaller to mid-sized acquisitions, we'd like to be at the run rate we pay for them within three years. That's a good deal for the shareholders and that's a good deal for all people involved."[25]

Implicit in the notion of addressing the future with your acquisitions in the present is taking a bit of a gamble on relatively new, unproven, small companies. That Cisco has done, by design, according to Cisco M&A chief Ammar Hanafi. "Large acquisitions are very hard to make work," he says. "There are lots of issues to focus on in terms of integration and capturing value." And small firms carry a beneficial kick in their typically higher-energy, go-for-broke culture. "We like to think of ourselves as the biggest start-up on the planet," Hanafi explains.[26]

CISCO'S KEY ELEMENTS IN ASSESSING ACQUISITIONS[27]

John Chambers lists five "rules of thumb" Cisco uses when sizing up a buying opportunity:

◆ *Shared vision.* "You've got to be in agreement with where you think the industry is going and what role each partner wants to play in that."

◆ *Cultural compatibility.* "If your cultures are different, they just never merge."

◆ *Geographic proximity.* Widely separated units may "never get the efficiencies" of having key people in a single location.

> ◆ **Short-term wins.** Acquired employees must quickly find benefits in acquisition.
>
> ◆ **Long-term wins.** Projections must show gains for all four of Cisco's key constituencies: shareholders, employees, customers, and business partners.

KNOW AND RESPECT THE DEAL KILLERS

Cisco's front-line tool for evaluating the advisability of an acquisition is its five "rules of thumb," which test for shared vision, cultural compatibility, geographic proximity, short-term wins for acquired employees, and long-term wins for all Cisco stakeholders. Chambers says that, in weighing a buying opportunity, "Anytime you don't have all five, it's a yellow light. And if you haven't got at least three of the five, you don't touch it. That has served us very well.

"We've killed nearly as many acquisitions as we have made," he adds, noting that, "It takes courage to walk. . . . You can actually get caught up in winning the acquisition rather than making the thing successful."

"It takes courage to walk. . . . You can actually get caught up in winning the acquisition rather than making the thing successful."

Compaq Computer's buyout of Digital Equipment Corporation, Chambers says, is a transaction that proceeded despite deal killers:

> They had different visions. They did not create the short-term wins for the people of the acquired company. The chemistries

and cultures were night and day in difference, and different geographic proximity. Four out of the five elements that we judge acquisitions on, they did not have.[28]

In knowing and respecting deal killers, and guarding constantly against getting caught up in making a deal for the sake of the deal, Cisco successfully contends with common attributes of acquisitions – such as the Compaq–DEC deal – that cause them to fail. These attributes are comprehensively summed up by A.T. Kearney consultant Douglas F. Aldrich, in his book *Mastering the Digital Marketplace*, as "The Seven Reasons Why Megamergers Do Not Work." They're condensed here, with comments added to suggest how Cisco avoids each pitfall:[29]

1. Firms join forces to exploit immature and inefficient markets, e.g. in the online market for information services, as illustrated by Compaq Computer's "squandering" the purchase of search engine Web portal Alta Vista.
   Comment: In the case of Cisco acquisitions, market presence is seldom a factor (most acquirees have little; Cisco has lots).

2. Regulatory changes often encourage corporations to merge or acquire as a hedge against uncertainty and in an attempt to control the market and defend their positions.
   Comment: No such changes appear to have influenced any Cisco acquisitions.

3. Companies demonstrate an apparent need to pressure suppliers and other third parties by consolidating and using economies of scale.
   Comment: Here, too, a non-issue for Cisco – unless perhaps "third parties" is broadened to include customers, some of

whom have expressed misgivings about Cisco being so dominant in its markets that it becomes the only practical choice as supplier.

4. Companies merge or acquire for access to physical assets.
   Comment: Cisco buys first for intellectual assets and second for future products; acquirees' current physical assets seem to have played little or no role in most acquisitions.

5. Firms can merge and acquire without exchanging cash, as in stock-for-stock deals.
   Comment: In a September 1999 review of Cisco's 10 most recent acquisitions, *CFO* magazine listed five as poolings of interests, four as stock purchases, and only one as a cash purchase – suggesting Cisco may be susceptible to this reason for M&A failure. But Cisco – with daily revenues of $40 million and a cash hoard reportedly amounting to $9 billion – could use cash flow to cover its deals.

6. Firms merge in an attempt to globalize operations.
   Comment: A non-issue with Cisco, which has long operated globally and prefers to buy locally – or at least domestically.

7. Consolidating operations appears to spread overhead costs over a greater number of revenue dollars. The aim of M&A should be strengthening the core activities.
   Comment: Cisco's acquisitions rarely add current revenue dollars of any significance to spreading overhead costs, and they aren't even considered if they don't strengthen core activities.

Testing Cisco with Aldrich's reasons for M&A failure indicates that the company's acquisitions have been made for right reasons, an opinion confirmed over time by the conclusions of analysts who closely watch Cisco's every move. Do your company's M&A ventures also pass the Aldrich test?

MAKE THEM AN OFFER THEY CAN'T REFUSE . . .

Cisco appears to make the buys it really wants by dispensing with gamesmanship and forthrightly valuing the qualities of a target acquisition that make it attractive. In reconstructing the events that culminated in Cisco's blockbuster $6.9 billion purchase of Cerent, *Business Week* reported that Chambers sat down with Cerent CEO Carl Russo during a technology conference "for a get-to-know-you":

> After a few pleasantries, Chambers got right to the point: "How much would it cost me to buy you?" he asked. . . . In the end, it seemed no price would dissuade Chambers. . . . To seal the deal, Chambers made a stunning concession: He told Russo that all personnel decisions about Cerent's workers would be made jointly by the two executives – forever.[30]

"How much would it cost for you to leave us alone?" – Cerent CEO Carl Russo's response to Chambers' initial acquisition inquiry

Chambers thus sets the everything- on-the-table tone of Cisco's negotiations to buy any company, regardless who takes the lead in face-to-face talks with the target. In a profile of Cisco business development VP Michelangelo Volpi, *The New York Times* described a meeting at which top executives of Lightspeed International, a maker of software to manage voice transmission over data networks, expected to discuss a licensing arrangement with Volpi:

> With the fresh backing of [Chambers], who had earlier op-
> posed a takeover of the company, Volpi cut right to the chase.
> Within three hours both sides had agreed to terms. And Light-
> speed's managers did not even bother to tell other suitors
> before the buyout was announced a week later. "We didn't
> feel the need to go to anyone else," said . . . Lightspeed's chief
> executive.[31]

Of course, Cisco uses more than a frank, unvarnished negotiat-
ing style and persistence to fashion deals that targets find
impossible to turn down. There's also the considerable lure of
Cisco stock, which *The New York Times* calls "one of the most
valuable currencies in the technology business today." In the
Lightspeed acquisition, the owners received shares worth $196
million when they completed the deal. Less than a year later,
their value exceeded $320 million.

And there's more, such as the opportunity Cisco provides to
put its name and global presence behind a startup's innovative
technology or product and launch it into the marketing strato-
sphere. Cisco senior VP Howard Charney, founder of Cisco
acquisition Grand Junction Networks, says the buyout provided "the chance to kick our products through the roof." *Inc.*
magazine reported that, "since the acquisition, sales of products derived from Grand Junction's former product line . . .
have mushroomed by a factor of eight, propelled by Cisco's
global marketing."[32]

. . . AND MAKE SURE YOU DELIVER AFTER THE DEAL

Cisco follows through on its pre-acquisition commitments –
even when they obligate the company in perpetuity – as is the
case in the Cerent deal's provision for joint personnel decisions. That provision is itself only a modification of what Cisco

calls the "Mario Rule" – named after Cisco senior VP Mario
Mazzola, formerly CEO of Cisco acquiree Crescendo Communications – which holds that any employee in a newly acquired
company can be terminated only with consent of both Chambers and the acquiree's former CEO. "It tells new employees
that Cisco wants them, that Cisco cares about them, and that
we're not just another big company," says Cisco legal and
government affairs VP Daniel Scheinman. "It buys the trust of
the people . . . and their passion is worth a lot more than any of
the downside legal protection."[33]

> "[Acquired
> employees
> have] got to see a
> future. They've got to
> see a culture they want
> to be a part of. They
> have got to see an
> opportunity to really
> do what they were
> doing before or
> even more."

Chambers wants acquired employees to be very happy
at Cisco – and he recognizes that takes work.
"How do you get the employees comfortable
so they want to be with that company
5 and 10 years later?" he asks himself.
"They've got to see a future. They've
got to see a culture they want to be a
part of. They have got to see an opportunity to really do what they
were doing before or even more."
Chambers is particularly attuned to
"maintaining two major groups – the
management teams and the engineers.
We track that very carefully."[34]

Clearly, the company's special efforts work. Vol-
untary attrition among acquired employees averages
6 percent annually, while comparable rates in other IT firms
exceed 40 percent. (See "How Cisco Keeps 'Acquired' Employees" in Chapter 4.)

It's clear that Cisco practices what Arthur D. Little consultants

Ronald S. Jonash and Tom Sommerlatte, in their book *The Innovation Premium*, call "integration by inclusion" – an alternative to a company's natural impulse "to integrate the newcomer into the culture and organization as quickly as possible" with tactics that fail "because they are top-down and thus reflexively resisted." Under integration by inclusion, on the other hand, the acquired company's workers are integrated into the acquiring company's existing learning network, "through which its workers can absorb the new technologies, processes, and culture *as members of a peer group, not as subordinates* [emphasis added]. The pride and confidence of the new workers are reinforced."[35]

> "[Cisco] has been phenomenally successful at holding on to the intellectual assets it buys."
>
> – *Business Week*

M&A consultant Mitchell Lee Marks, coauthor of *Joining Forces: Making One Plus One Equal Three in Mergers, Acquisitions, and Alliances*, also warns against impatience in attempts to meld two companies into one following a combination. "What's most required from top executives is patience," he says. "But the top people often feel pressured to immediately begin realizing the synergies that a combination is supposed to bring. . . . Senior executives may not realize that the months of negotiation have given them time to adapt, but their employees have had no time at all."

Time is needed, he says, "because just about anyone affected by a merger or buyout tends to look at the glass as half empty. It's more the uncertainties than the realities of the combination that cause people to fear it." Helping employees overcome fear, Marks says, "involves actions that are probably about two-thirds just good, sound management. But the other one-third are actions unique to a merger." That's because you're running the organization along two tracks: managing the merger and simultaneously managing the ongoing business. "So even the best-run combinations are characterized by two steps forward and one back," Marks says. "You're telling people, 'This will be tough sledding, but we'll get through it and be stronger than ever.'"[36]

Cisco has repeatedly gotten stronger than ever through its string of acquisitions, and shows no sign of slowing down. "We will acquire probably 10 to 15 companies a year," Chambers says. "[T]here are so many areas in this market that no one company can address it by themselves."[37]

BUY RIGHT TO GROW LIKE GANGBUSTERS

The ever-lengthening record of failures among corporate mergers and acquisitions proves that there's a wrong way to merge or buy; Cisco's lengthening record of buyouts that benefit everyone involved indicates there's a right way, too. Here are key elements of acquisition success:

◆ *Buy to keep moving at Internet speed.* No one company, on its own, can keep up with the pace of change required today for continuing success over time. Acquisitions can bring change into the organization.

◆ *Make people the primary purpose.* The products and technologies of an acquisition target shouldn't be the foremost concerns of your evaluation. What counts above all else is the pool of talent you could add to your roster; only people have a value that can justify a rich purchase price.

◆ *Don't sweat the present, buy the future.* Some of Cisco's deals have looked downright foolish on paper – premium prices for enterprises not yet out of diapers. But Cisco isn't paying for what was or is, but what will be. That approach, more often than not, will lead to acquisitions that prove to be well worth the outlay made to seal the deal.

◆ *Know and respect the deal killers.* John Chambers is wary of deals pursued to completion for the sake of completing the deal. Formulate and rigidly enforce your key criteria for going through with a deal; when signs don't say "go," stop.

◆ *Make them an offer they can't refuse.* Cisco is known and respected for fairly valuing the companies it targets for acquisition and not letting minor hitches get in the way of reaching agreement. That's a big plus with stakeholders in the target outfit.

◆ *. . . and make sure you deliver after the deal.* Cisco's integration of acquired companies is famously fair to new employees. They respond favorably to strong inducements to stay – and make Cisco's rate of retaining acquired employees by far the best among high-tech firms.

NOTES

1. Holson, Laura M., "Whiz Kid: Young Deal Maker Is the Force Behind a Company's Growth," *New York Times*, 19 November 1998.

2. Jonash, Ronald S., and Sommerlatte, Tom, *The Innovation Premium: How Next-Generation Companies Are Achieving Peak Performance and Profitability*, Perseus, Cambridge, Massachusetts, 1999.

3. Donnelly, George, "Acquiring Minds," *CFO*, 1 September 1999.

4. Daly, James, "The Art of the Deal," *Business 2.0*, October 1999.

5. Author interview.

6. Donnelly, George, "Acquiring Minds," *CFO*, 1 September 1999.

7. Donnelly, George, "Acquiring Minds," *CFO*, 1 September 1999.

8. Schlender, Brent, "The Real Road Ahead," *Fortune*, 25 October 1999.

9. Daly, James, "The Art of the Deal," *Business 2.0*, October 1999.

10. Compiled from numerous reports.

11. Albrecht, Karl, *Corporate Radar*, Amacom, New York, 2000.

12. Port, Otis, "Customers Move Into the Driver's Seat," *Business Week*, 4 October 1999.

13. Donnelly, George, "Acquiring Minds," *CFO*, 1 September 1999.

14. Daly, James, "The Art of the Deal," *Business 2.0*, October 1999.

15. Goldblatt, Henry, "Cisco's Secrets," *Fortune*, 8 November 1999.

16. Holson, Laura M., "Whiz Kid: Young Deal Maker Is the Force Behind a Company's Growth," *New York Times*, 19 November 1998.

17. Daly, James, "The Art of the Deal," *Business 2.0*, October 1999.

18. Ferguson, Charles H., *High Stakes, No Prisoners*, Times Business, New York, 1999.

19. Byrne, John, "The Corporation of the Future," *Business Week*, 24 August 1998.

20. Donnelly, George, "Acquiring Minds," *CFO*, 1 September 1999.

21. Thurm, Scott, "Cisco to Acquire Networking Firm Cerent," *Wall Street Journal*, 26 August 1999.

22. McCarthy, Jack, and Heichler, Elizabeth, "Cisco Boosts Optical-Networking Presence," *InfoWorld*, 30 August 1999.

23. Donnelly, George, "Acquiring Minds," *CFO*, 1 September 1999.

24. Byrne, John, "The Corporation of the Future," *Business Week*, 24 August 1998.

25. Daly, James, "The Art of the Deal," *Business 2.0*, October 1999.

26. Donnelly, George, "Acquiring Minds," *CFO*, 1 September 1999.

27. Daly, James, "The Art of the Deal," *Business 2.0*, October 1999.

28. Daly, James, "The Art of the Deal," *Business 2.0*, October 1999.

29. Aldrich, Douglas F., *Mastering the Digital Marketplace*, John Wiley & Sons, New York, 1999.

30. Reinhardt, Andy, "The Man Who Hones Cisco's Cutting Edge, *Business Week*, 13 September 1999.

31. Holson, Laura M., "Whiz Kid: Young Deal Maker Is the Force Behind a Company's Growth," *New York Times*, 19 November 1998.

32. Plotkin, Hal, "Cisco's Secret: Entrepreneurs Sell Out, Stay Put," *Inc.*, March 1997.

33. Byrne, John, "The Corporation of the Future," *Business Week*, 24 August 1998.

34. Daly, James, "The Art of the Deal," *Business 2.0*, October 1999.

35. Jonash, Ronald S., and Sommerlatte, Tom, *The Innovation Premium*, Perseus, Cambridge, Massachusetts, 1999.

36. Author interview.

37. CNNfn, "Market Coverage," 26 August 1999.

Nine

IF YOU DON'T BUY 'EM, JOIN 'EM

IN THIS CHAPTER

The central feature of Cisco's horizontal business model is alliance with other firms to the benefit of all participants. Cisco has its own ways of making strategic partnerships work; they're described in this chapter.

Cisco Systems twice made headlines in August 1999 by announcing mega-partnerships:

◆ Early in the month, Cisco and accounting–consulting giant KPMG Peat Marwick revealed they would ally to help telecommunications service providers and big companies deliver Internet-based services.

◆ Later, Cisco and IBM announced a multifaceted cooperative arrangement under which the two giant tech firms essentially agreed to bring years of scrapping and sniping to a screeching halt and link arms to – as Cisco senior VP Selby Wellman put it – "give both companies more access to each other's customers and markets."[1]

What's remarkable here? Not that former competitors are co-operating. Intel chairman Andy Grove says, "It's not clear anymore who you need to be at loggerheads with."[2]

What's most remarkable about these alliances – other than the prominence of the firms involved and the size of the deals – is how unremarkable they are. Because if you had to come up with a one-word characterization of the 1990s in business, you could make a good case for calling it the alliance decade. "Corporate alliances are taking the world by storm," says an article in the September 1998 issue of *Strategy & Leadership* magazine.[3] "The world is just a whirl of alliances," begins an October 1999 special report in *Business Week*.[4] True, to say the least, considering that a single company, such as Oracle, might have

15,000 or more partnerships at once. (The business press and this book use "partnership" and "alliance" interchangeably.)

> "Our business model has always been heavily weighted toward business partners. Alliances . . . are the secret to success." – Cisco senior VP Selby Wellman

Cisco seems not to be distinguished in the world of alliances by its number of such relationships, but the company excels in making them work. "Our business model has always been heavily weighted toward business partners," Wellman observes. "Alliances like this are the secret to success. You'll see more things along this line."[5]

WHY ALLIANCES ARE HOT[6]

Business Week says business alliances have recently soared in popularity because:

◆ companies can stick to their "core competencies" while offering customers a broader range of products and services;

◆ complementary operations, such as production and distribution, can be mixed and matched;

◆ they can be put together fast and dismantled relatively simply;

◆ the Internet and other emerging technologies require a level of corporate nimbleness that partnerships can provide;

◆ they offer an avenue for non-global firms to achieve relatively quick, inexpensive worldwide reach;

◆ they allow firms to share risk, particularly in projects that are becoming too big and complex for even billion-dollar companies to take on alone;

◆ US antitrust watchdogs are generally adopting a hands-off posture toward them.

DON'T GO IT ALONE

Renowned author, soldier, and hunter Ernest Hemingway – whose life and works have been said by some to represent the epitome of independent action – wrote, "A man alone ain't got no chance."

That thought could as well express circumstances for companies, even the largest global outfits, in the Internet-speed world of the early 21st century. "We're in the midst of a sea change," says John Chambers. "The Internet has transformed the IT industries from a collection of oligopolies into a more diverse ecosystem in which the important thing isn't so much what technologies you own as how well you can work with the other players." Partnering participation is neither optional nor easy, Chambers contends. "We don't have a choice. It'll be a challenge because partnerships are more difficult to manage than acquisitions."[7]

He's got that right. Yale management professor Barry J. Nalebuff, author of the book *Co-opetition*, says alliances entered into with the best of win-win intentions more often than not spiral downward to lose-lose outcomes. "More interrelationships mean more conflicts of interest," he says, "along with more divorces – and custody battles." Research indicates that more than half of all corporate alliances fail outright or hobble along with no benefits for participants.[8]

So why bother? Because research also shows big benefits from partnering. A Coopers & Lybrand study showed that firms involved in alliances had 11 percent higher revenue and a 20 percent higher growth rate than companies not engaged in alliance activity.[9] Andersen Consulting claims that alliances will represent $25–40 trillion in value by 2004. The company says that the average large company went from no alliances in 1989 to 30-plus in 1999.[10] Cisco's Selby Wellman boils down the alliance imperative to a single direct statement: "No one company can keep up with an industry that's moving at warp speed."[11]

A Coopers & Lybrand study showed that firms involved in alliances had 11 percent higher revenue and a 20 percent higher growth rate than companies not engaged in alliance activity.

Partnering consultant Jordan D. Lewis, author most recently of *Trusted Partners: How Companies Build Mutual Trust and Win Together*, offers this alliance stunner: Chrysler [now Daimler–Chrysler], which had no alliance with suppliers in 1990, "achieved more than $500 million in savings proposed by suppliers in the 1994 model year alone. Because about 69 percent of the total cost of producing Chrysler's cars are managed by suppliers, these savings were a major reason why Chrysler achieved lowest costs and highest profits per vehicle in North America."

What are the key characteristics of alliances that produce such dramatic results? Alliances, Lewis asserts, "are sustained by mutual need, a common objective seen as important enough to dominate any issue, a willingness to share the benefits, and a trusting relationship." You've got to make them happen, he contends, because "the demands on individual firms have become too vast to be met by each one acting in isolation."[12]

WHY ALLY?[13]

Grant Gisel, who heads IT consulting firm Sierra Systems Consultants Inc., lists "three major reasons for getting involved in alliances":

◆ To try and provide a better, improved service to our clients. We look at relationships with other companies as a way of bringing a bigger package together, a more complete solution than we could provide independently.

◆ By partnering with others, we've been able to build a team that could take on much larger assignments than we would have been able – or would have been prudent financially – to take on by ourselves.

◆ Alliances have provided better opportunities for our staff in terms of diversity, challenge, and complexity of assignments.

"So [alliance] is better for the client, better for our staff, and certainly it's been an integral part of Sierra's growth."

HAVE THE COURAGE TO FORM "INTERWOVEN DEPENDENCIES"

Cisco's annual report states that the open nature of the emerging Internet ecosystem encourages "complementary business alliances that create a unique set of interwoven dependencies and relationships."

The most consequential words in this statement are "unique"

and "interwoven," because they hint at one of the overriding facts of life in strategic partnering: no optimally effective alliance can be based in its entirety on a written agreement. To a greater or lesser extent, every mutually beneficial partnership will be based on trust.

"In an alliance, you can't define every detail," Jordan Lewis writes in *Trusted Partners.* "Success depends on creatively joining the ideas and energies of two firms, sometimes more. . . . Alliances are framed by an understanding that it is in neither firm's interest to hurt the other. Most important of all, alliances depend on trust. No contract can anticipate what two groups must do to be creative together."[14]

Trust is the foremost distinction between what John Chambers might think of as a straightforward, "old world" transaction and a creative, multifaceted, "new world" alliance. Lewis says supplier alliances replace "traditional arm's-length relationships," which are "confined to an exchange of terms." In transactions, the buyer's task was seen as one of "forcing suppliers to take risks alone and demanding price concessions and other actions that weaken suppliers' commitments and even the [buying] firms themselves." Lewis contrasts such "narrow relationships" with true alliances, in which purchasers, "working with suppliers to create unique value, add [those suppliers] to a firm's distinct competitive resources."[15]

In his book *Partnering Intelligence: Creating Value for Your Business by Building Strong Alliances*, partnership consultant Stephen M. Dent offers three criteria that make trust – and, therefore, effective alliances – possible:

◆ *Telling the truth* – means facing up to reality, telling the whole story, not putting a spin on important matters. Admit mistakes, acknowledge weaknesses, and ask for help.

◆ *Taking the time* – to build a relationship. Trust is the result of time we spend building it; it can't be wished onto a relationship.

◆ *Being accountable* – relates to your own actions. You can't control what someone else does, but you can control what you do. The law of reciprocity – others give back what they've been given – works in building trusting relationships.

Cisco literally thrives on the trust it has built with partners and all of its varied constituencies. For example, the company's enterprise marketing group seeks to serve as a "strategic" supplier for its top 100–500 accounts – defining "strategic" as having gained enough trust from a customer for Cisco to be included in the customer's network planning and purchasing.[17]

KEYS TO SUCCESSFUL PARTNERING[18]

Alliance consultant Larraine Segil, author of the book *Intelligent Business Alliances*, directed a study of partnering from which she derived keys to success that include the following:

◆ *Common culture is key to alliance success.* Seventy-five percent of some 200 companies surveyed felt that alliance failure was caused by incompatibility of corporate cultures or personalities.

◆ *Tiering is an effective method of organizing large volumes of alliances.* Dividing alliances into tiers, ranked by the importance of each partnership to the company, means the company can disperse capital and resources to each tier according to its value.

◆ **Open communication between alliance partners is essential.** Starbucks' policy of informal communication with its strategic partners is simple and straightforward: "We pick up the telephone and talk."

◆ **Monitoring customer responses and service complaints helps ensure success.** A successful alliance depends on the partners' ability to sustain "customer" satisfaction.

◆ **Managing the collaboration/competition dilemma is vital.** Oracle partners in some areas with companies that are competitors in other areas, but also constructs "firewalls" to ensure the competitive and cooperative units don't mix.

◆ **Flexibility throughout the alliance relationship is key.** Defining specific criteria for alliances is essential, but they are most effective when specific issues are addressed on a case-by-case basis.

◆ **Measuring, monitoring, and reviewing must continue throughout the life of the alliance.** That means establishing criteria for success of the partnership at the outset.

CREATE WINS FOR OTHERS TO WIN BIG YOURSELF

As a vocal disciple of the so-called horizontal business model –

"I cannot afford to compete with my partners."

under which a company reaches out to establish mutually beneficial relationships with many other companies – John Chambers has this to say about why he doesn't create a "vertical" internal structure to address every new development in networking: "I cannot afford to compete with my partners."[19]

And Cisco's partners appreciate that. Says Michael R. Rich,

who heads Cisco partner NetSpeak: "What they do is create an environment that lets smaller companies like Net-Speak innovate. . . . We're able to do that as an added-value sale on top of a Cisco network. . . . We support strongly Cisco's strategy for an ecosystem; it's going to make them look like the Microsoft of networking."[20]

> "What [Cisco does] is create an environment that lets smaller companies like NetSpeak innovate." – NetSpeak chief Michael R. Rich

True, except that Cisco extends its brand of partnering to every corner of the company. For example, Del Dameron, with the law firm of McKenna & Cuneo, says,

> Our partnership relationship has fostered a greater sense of commitment to the client. It is important to understand that this whole partnering concept for Cisco is by no means limited to their outside law firms. They apply it across the board to accounting firms, suppliers, other high-tech companies. Their corporate culture seeks these types of win–win relationships for everyone involved. It is very much a two-way street, and we feel very fortunate to be a part of it.[21]

The implications of failing to seek wins for your partners might be seen in looking at the early days of another Internet legend, Netscape, as described by Michael Cusumano and David B. Yoffie in *Competing on Internet Time: Lessons from Netscape and its Battle with Microsoft*. The big problem with Netscape as a corporate partner, they write:

> . . . was [Netscape's] philosophy and its failure to devote resources to partnering. [CEO] Marc Andreessen . . . sought customers, not partners. In his words, "Having a partnership or a partner relationship without having some economic benefit flowing one way or another is nothing – it doesn't count." This

attitude was understandable in a start-up hungry for cash, but it was also dangerous in a world where competitors – such as Microsoft – took a very different approach. Microsoft lavished time, money, and support on companies, such as applications developers, that were aligned with its interests. By contrast, . . . Netscape tries to suck every dollar they can out of the Web.[22]

Cisco, with its concern for seeing that partners win in their Cisco relationships, creates wins for itself. Or, in colloquial terms, "What goes around, comes around." Focusing on creating wins for others is the only route to realizing sustained wins for yourself. In *Partnering Intelligence*, Stephen M. Dent writes, "Those who believe their interests are being addressed feel valued and important. They feel part of a team, and they'll invest their time and energy in helping the team succeed. . . . If your partner loses independence or can't maintain a separate identity, your partnership ceases to exist."[23]

Similarly, consultant Jordan Lewis says this about supplier alliances: "The goal is to improve together, rather than alone; to earn supplier loyalty by focusing on underlying costs while protecting *suppliers'* [emphasis added] margins." He notes that companies known for all-around excellence, such as Motorola and British retailer Marks & Spencer, "strive to be their suppliers' best customer." They even monitor suppliers' financial health, because "they want suppliers to remain strong, invest for the future, and stay committed to [partnership] objectives."[24]

SIX PATHS TO PARTNERSHIP PAIN[25]

Every partnership involves at least a little pain, say consultants Chip Bell of Performance Research Associates and Heather Shea of Interim

Career Counseling, in their book *Dance Lessons: Six Steps to Great Partnerships in Business and Life*. But it's smart to avoid prospective partnerships that could create more than a little pain. Here are six warning signs:

◆ *Everyone's doing it.* Given the popularity of alliances, some of them are created more for show than function.

◆ *Trust me!* Beware a hard sell, especially from a potential partner whose resources and talents don't balance yours. Watch out for glowing generalizations. Good feelings should be based on a realistic assessment of potential success.

◆ *'Till death do us part.* Unrealistic expectations about the longevity of a partnership can cause partners to miss the cues for a graceful exit.

◆ *The one-night stand.* A once-only transaction is not a partnership. Despite the current rhetoric, a customer is not a partner, nor is a single-transaction vendor.

◆ *Organ donor needed.* Some potential partners assume that allying with a healthy partner is a great way to get a caregiver. The result is usually an unwell partnership.

◆ *Blind loyalty.* The ad agency, banker, or consultant you keep around unquestioningly, year after year, can be a sign of stagnation.

USE ALLIANCE LEVERAGE TO MOVE FASTER

To keep your company moving at Internet speed – in other words, to survive in the 21st century – alliances are an imperative, not an option. With well-run alliances, a company can extend its virtual reach just about anywhere it wishes to go. Example: Cisco's stated intention to rely increasingly on partners such as KPMG Consulting and value-added resellers to generate sales. To make that happen, Cisco has given its sales-people incentives to direct customer orders to Cisco partners, according to executive VP Gary Dai-chendt. Today, "over 80 percent of our business is fulfilled through our partners," he says.[26]

"Over 80 percent of our business is fulfilled through our partners." – Cisco executive VP Gary Daichendt

That leverages sales. Cisco also uses alliances to leverage time. "Partners collapse time because they allow you to take on more things and bring them together quicker," says executive VP Don Listwin. Example: Cisco's partnership with Microsoft, which resulted in a new technology to make networks more intelligent. "From initial discussion to technology, it took 18 months to get the product out," says Listwin. Alone, "it would have taken us four years to get to where we are, and it's not clear we had the competence to get there alone."[27]

"Partners collapse time because they allow you to take on more things and bring them together quicker." – Cisco executive VP Don Listwin

Cisco leverages alliances to the point that it won't launch an internal unit aimed at accomplishing something that a partner can do better. Recall that John Chambers says he won't compete with partners. That approach is encouraged by Jordan Lewis. In *Trusted Partners*, he argues that

. . . seeking help from others only after concluding you can't do something alone is shortsighted. . . . There is a better approach. To appreciate it, ask yourself the following: Can your company, on its own, be at the cutting edge in all it must do? Probably not. So consider this: In a world rich in advancing know-how, why not assess the resources and know-how of other firms that might add value to yours, before your plans are set? . . . Said differently, your customers and stockholders don't care where you get your ideas, products, or technology. What keeps them on board is that your firm brings them more value sooner than others.[28]

ALLY OR ACQUIRE?[29]

Business Week says alliances can sometimes make more sense than acquisitions because partnering can provide:

◆ flexibility and informality that promote efficiencies;

◆ ready access to new markets and technologies;

◆ the ability to create and disband projects with minimum paperwork;

◆ shared risks and expenses;

◆ retained independent brand identification;

◆ synergies in working with partners possessing multiple skills;

◆ a way for rivals to work harmoniously together;

◆ multifarious forms, from simple R&D deals to huge projects;

◆ capacity for participation by dozens of participants; and

◆ shelter from antitrust laws for cooperative R&D activities.

IF YOU DON'T BUY 'EM, JOIN 'EM

Strategic alliances can provide a way for your company to significantly extend its reach to new technologies, markets, and customers. But they only work with the sort of commitment and hard work that Cisco brings to bear, observing these most important guidelines:

◆ **Don't go it alone.** The leveraging that can result from smart partnering not only makes them advisable, but increasingly a necessity. The pressures of continual change, global competition, and shifting customer demands can no longer be adequately addressed by any single organization; alliance is often an effective response.

◆ **Have the courage to form "interwoven dependencies."** The way a beneficial partnership will evolve over time can't be detailed in advance – it must be flexible enough to respond quickly to a changing environment. That makes trust the essential element of alliances that succeed.

◆ **Create wins for others to win big yourself.** Alliances are in trouble when any participant seeks to gain more than partners from the arrangement. Look for ways your partners can benefit from their alliance with you – which, paradoxically, better ensures your own gains.

◆ **Use alliance leverage to move faster.** Partnerships, like acquisitions, can provide a way for companies to respond proactively to the accelerating pace of change. Continuing growth is the key promise in alliance, your firm joins others to exploit complementary competencies and access to each others' markets and customers.

NOTES

1. Uncredited, "Cisco Sends IBM $2 Billion Deal For Chips, Parts," *San Francisco Chronicle*, 1 September 1999.

2. Schlender, Brent, "The Real Road Ahead," *Fortune*, 25 October 1999.

3. Segil, Larraine, "Strategic Alliances for the 21st Century," *Strategy & Leadership*, 1 September 1998.

4. Sparks, Debra, "Partners," *Business Week*, 25 October 1999.

5. Uncredited, "IBM, Cisco Create Powerful Team for E-business Networks," *Electronic Commerce News*, 6 September 1999.

6. Sparks, Debra, "Partners," *Business Week*, 25 October 1999.

7. Schlender, Brent, "The Real Road Ahead," *Fortune*, 25 October 1999.

8. Sparks, Debra, "Partners," *Business Week*, 25 October 1999.

9. Segil, Larraine, "Strategic Alliances for the 21st Century," *Strategy & Leadership*, 1 September 1998.

10. Sparks, Debra, "Partners," *Business Week*, 25 October 1999.

11. Hersch, Warren S., "IBM Exits Networking Market in Big Cisco Deal," *Computer Reseller News*, 6 September 1999.

12. Author interview.

13. Cyr, Dianne, "Sierra Systems' CEO Grant Gisel on High Technology Alliances," *Academy of Management Executive*, May 1999.

14. Lewis, Jordan D., *Trusted Partners: How Companies Build Mutual Trust and Win Together*, Free Press, New York, 2000.

15. Author interview.

16. Dent, Stephen M., *Partnering Intelligence*, Davies-Black, Palo Alto, California, 1999.

17. Duffy, Jim, "Cisco Has a New Name for its Top Customers: 'Strategic,'" *Network World*, 4 November 1996.

18. Segil, Larraine, "Strategic Alliances for the 21st Century," *Strategy & Leadership*, 1 September 1998.

19. Janah, Monua, "Computer-Networking Firms Seek to Boost Sales," *San Jose Mercury News*, 11 August 1999.

20. Uncredited, "Breaking Out of the In Pack," *Intelligent Network News*, 13 October 1999.

21. Uncredited, "Focus On: Partnering – McKenna & Cuneo and Cisco Systems Model an Effective Partnering Relationship," *Metropolitan Corporate Counsel*, September 1999.

22. Cusumano, Michael, and Yoffie, David B., *Competing on Internet Time*, Free Press, New York, 1998.

23. Dent, Stephen M., *Partnering Intelligence*, Davies-Black, Palo Alto, California, 1999.

24. Author interview.

25. Bell, Chip R., and Shea, Heather, *Dance Lessons: Six Steps to Great Partnerships in Business and Life*, Berrett-Koehler, San Francisco, 1998.

26. Janah, Monua, "Computer-Networking Firms Seek to Boost Sales," *San Jose Mercury News*, 11 August 1999.

27. Byrne, John, "The Corporation of the Future," *Business Week*, 24 August 1998.

28. Lewis, Jordan D., *Trusted Partners: How Companies Build Mutual Trust and Win Together*, Free Press, New York, 2000.

29. Sparks, Debra, "Partners," *Business Week*, 25 October 1999.

Ten

FIGHT COMPLACENCY THAT CAN ACCOMPANY SUCCESS

IN THIS CHAPTER

John Chambers learned how complacency can bring down seemingly invincible companies during his years at IBM and Wang. So he leads Cisco into the competitive fray each day as if the company were still that precarious start-up operating out of the founders' living room. The principles discussed in this chapter help ward off any temptation toward corporate complacency.

D espite leading Cisco to growth unequaled in world business history, John Chambers is not quite ready to sit back, kick off his shoes, and light a victory cigar. In fact, it's safe to say such a sight is unlikely to be seen before Halley's Comet once again streaks into view from earth (in the latter part of the 21st century).

Chambers understands that there's no ultimate "victory" in the new economy; there is only having the strength to battle another day. He says, "Anybody who doesn't think they're vulnerable in this new economy or that their implementation can't go awry, doesn't get it."[1] That statement speaks volumes about Chambers' extreme aversion to resting on his laurels – or, for that matter, even pausing to catch his breath.

REMEMBER PAST SUCCESS – IS PAST

John Chambers and his top team run Cisco as if they were always thinking about that boilerplate statement that accompanies investment pitches: Past performance is not an indicator of future success. Chambers expresses constant trepidation, as if he suspects that the more successful he is, the greater failure he might someday become. "Cisco could be a non-major factor within one to two years if we misstep," he says.[2] Other times, he's more optimistic: "There is the realization that you can be out of business in three years."[3]

But business history, littered with great falls of the once high and mighty, proves the merit of the Chambers outlook. In more than a few instances – General Motors, Sears, and IBM (*see boxed sidebar*) among them – long ascents to apparent invincibility seem only to expose a firm to the law of regression to the mean: a string of bad years that offset the good. *Investor's Business Daily* recently recalled that in the late 1980s, "Digital Equipment chief Ken Olsen scoffed at the idea of putting personal computers in every household. At about the same time, two 'All-Pro' brokers in *Money*'s survey named Digital a buy. But Olsen's firm slumped in the '90s and is now a division of PC maker Compaq Computer."[4] One imagines that would be a fate worse than death for John Chambers.

And also for Marshall Industries CEO Robert Rodin. In *Free, Perfect, and Now: Connecting to the Three Insatiable Customer Demands*, he states that today no company, no matter how successful, can afford to rest on its laurels:

> The pace of marketplace change constantly accelerates, so we will have to learn to change faster, too, or risk losing everything we've built. Survival is not mandated for any of us, individually or collectively; we have to earn it. Where can we connect with our future? What are the barriers to free, perfect, and now? How can we get past them?[5]

Creating a culture in which a company keeps coming up with the best answers to those questions, Rodin writes, "isn't about building a kinder, gentler workplace; it's about building a more competitive team. The more curiosity we bring to the world and the better we learn to listen to problems, the more innovative solutions we can develop – and innovation . . . represents our only hope for a future."

LOU BRINGS "BIG BLUE" BACK FROM THE BRINK[6]

The notion that success breeds success was deep-sixed by IBM's storied fall from the pinnacle. "By 1993, IBM . . . seemed on the verge of falling apart," writes Robert Slater, in his book *Saving Big Blue: Leadership Lessons and Turnaround Tactics of IBM's Lou Gerstner.* The company's board, turned down in its CEO search by many leaders in the technology sector, hired then-RJR Nabisco CEO Louis V. Gerstner Jr. "Today . . . no one denies that Gerstner has performed the miracle that everyone thought was impossible." How did he do it? Slater says Gerstner's arsenal included the following:

◆ *Gerstner lowered expectations.* "When Gerstner suggested to analysts that he really possessed no grand vision for the company," Slater writes, "he only served to reinforce their original fears that he was not up to the job."

◆ *He came in with the customer's perspective.* Gerstner took the helm at IBM after many years as an IBM customer.

◆ *He learned before he acted.* Gerstner started off slowly in his new position, "trying to learn the ropes first before making major decisions."

◆ *He preferred small steps to dramatic changes.* Unlike many brash turnaround executives, Gerstner "was ready to play the role of tinkerer. He wanted no wholesale revolutions at IBM."

◆ *He danced with the ones that brung him.* Gerstner rejected recommendations that he abandon IBM's mainframe and/or PC products. The reason: "to convince customers that Big Blue was the best place to do one-stop computer shopping."

◆ *But he also looked to new markets.* While sticking with its past winners, Gerstner also saw that "there was a growing amount of business to be won in the service realm."

> ◆ *He recognized the new role of sales reps.* Gerstner "required of his
> sales force that it not push products down customers' throats,"
> but rather work with them as problem-solving consultants.

MAKE EXPERIENCE YOUR FAVORITE
TEACHER

John Chambers readily acknowledges that IBM and Wang
Laboratories Inc. made him the CEO he is today. Usually left
unspoken, however, is the fact that in his stints with these firms
Chambers learned much about how *not* to run a company – for
his years with each outfit were those in which they fell igno-
miniously from former glory.

London's *Daily Telegraph* says Chambers' IBM and Wang years
"left him with a deep insecurity . . . haunted by the past." Not
so much haunted, it would seem, as guided – particularly by
the experience at Wang of wave after wave of layoffs, which
called for Chambers to dismiss a good-sized company's worth
of employees. "Nothing hurts you more than laying someone
off," he says. "At Wang, it was mismanagement, mis-executing.
I had to fire 5,000 people. That hurts. It was unbelievable."[7]

Then again, "haunted" may not be off the mark, if Chambers'
own father's words are on target. The retired doctor recalls the
rising executive's phone calls during those dark days at Wang:
"And he was miserable. And he would call home, and we
would talk about it, talk to his mother as well as to me, just explaining how difficult that was for him to do."[8]

Chambers says he couldn't have tolerated another year under

such conditions. He resigned from Wang in 1990 and joined Cisco the next year. But he credits his time with IBM and Wang for instilling in him a "healthy" paranoia – "the realization that if your company does not keep up, if you don't keep up as a leader, you hurt everyone: your customers, your shareholders, your employees, and your partners. I am just not going to do that again."[9]

> "If you don't keep up as a leader, you hurt everyone: your customers, your shareholders, your employees, and your partners. I am just not going to do that again."

While those Wang layoffs were surely the defining event of Chambers' pre-Cisco work life, those years just as surely presented Chambers with experiences he would gradually mold into a world view that would valuably inform his leadership of Cisco. What IT company other than IBM better embodies the era of the man in the grey flannel suit, where strict respect for corporate hierarchy and going along to get along were qualities held in higher regard than probing inquiry and original thinking? First-hand experience with failure of the IBM way at the dawn of the information age could only have aided his journey to the Cisco way as the information revolution exploded.

Other truths of managing in the Internet-speed world similarly have been drawn by Chambers from his IBM and Wang years:

◆ His "horizontal model" would rise where hierarchy crumbled.

◆ In the place where corporate self-sufficiency was once honored, he would find strength in an "ecosystem" of suppliers, customers, and partners.

◆ And the drive for stability as the ultimate corporate virtue would be replaced by recognition of constant change.

In short, it's unlikely that John Chambers would have succeeded as he has at Cisco, had he not gone through those "unbelievable" times at IBM and Wang.

A MAN WHO MAKES EXPERIENCE MEAN SOMETHING[10]

Every manager who rises through positions of increasing responsibility uses past experience to inform current actions. John Chambers seems to have put experience to work more effectively than most leaders – and become a legend in doing so.

Where Chambers is a record setter in leading corporate growth, Harold M. Williams may be the top manager of our time in terms of the variety of organizations he has led. Management and leadership guru Warren Bennis tabs Williams "a great success story, maybe the greatest, considering the vastly different spheres of the groups he's headed."[11] Williams launched his working career with food company Norton Simon Inc. After ascending to chairmanship there, he became dean of UCLA's Graduate School of Management, then head of the Securities and Exchange Commission, then president of the J. Paul Getty Trust.

What did he take with him in a career that crossed boundaries of business, academia, government, and the arts? Here are some key elements of the Williams experience:

◆ In all of his varied posts, Williams says, "I saw myself in essentially the same way. I am a manager of people. They know their subject matter better than I. They have their own vision, and they have the motivation that drives toward that vision."

◆ "I realized, early on, that good leadership means giving such people plenty of room. That made trust the most important attribute required of me in any of those jobs. Trust that they'll do what's right and best, and that they'll be straight with me."

◆ "I didn't take any new job without at least a hypothesis on how it might be done better. When I went from Norton Simon to UCLA, I had ideas for turning the school around in certain ways, because I had hired many MBAs and seen blind spots in their world view."

◆ "I knew I couldn't do anything alone." So, Williams recounts, he never went into a job and announced changes he determined unilaterally. "At UCLA, I had learned by talking to faculty members before I took the job that many of them agreed with some of the changes I thought might be needed."

◆ Although he closely examined every new opportunity before accepting it, Williams acknowledges that, "It was impossible to remove all the risk of making a change. And I wouldn't want to. If there were no risk, why would anyone want to make a change?"

EMBRACE PARANOIA

At IBM, where John Chambers got his start in business, company founder Thomas Watson was known for the "Think" motto that graced his office wall. Light years from Watson's imperative is the thought popularized by Intel Chairman Andy Grove: "Only the paranoid survive." The vast distance – not in miles or years, but in perspective – from Watson to Grove is created by the difference in self-image: confidence to the point of arrogance is replaced by self-doubt to the point of paranoia.

And John Chambers claims, with almost perverse pride, that Cisco rivals Intel in the paranoia department. "We make Andy Grove look positively placid," he says. He's supported in that claim by network research consultant Virginia Brooks, who says the Chambers quality that most impresses her "is that he really seems to understand he's got to keep this kind of healthy paranoia going. He knows that if Cisco ever gets too complacent, that it could end up as another Digital [Equipment] or another IBM."[12]

> "[Chambers] knows that if Cisco ever gets too complacent, that it could end up as another Digital or another IBM." – consultant Virginia Brooks

Forbes magazine views the same Chambers attribute in more stark terms, observing that, "Chambers is still scared. Very scared. That's because Chambers is a veteran of (gulp) Wang and IBM. So he's keenly aware of what it's like to be on top and then lose it all. 'People remember you for how you end up. That's an important paranoia to have,' he says."[13]

> "People remember you for how you end up. That's an important paranoia to have.

Of course paranoia that serves no constructive purpose might send Chambers to a shrink's couch rather than the covers of business publications around the world. But there's method to his madness, as he reveals in this rambling, but telling, comment:

> We have an unusual culture of being paranoid and worrying about everything and all the things that can trip us up and the confidence that if we execute right, listen to our customers, and motivate our people, that we potentially could be one of the most influential companies in the world.[14]

Anyone's list of influential companies would have to include Microsoft, of course, headed by a man who is credited with a case of corporate paranoia that's as serious as Chambers' or Grove's. In *Hard Drive: Bill Gates and the Making of the Microsoft Empire,* authors James Wallace and Jim Erickson report that Bill Gates "is always looking over his shoulder." The idea that Gates will forever be watching his back is conveyed by the Gates quote that concludes the book: "I look out there and see fun people to work with, who are learning a lot. That's cool, and that feels good, but we're not on top. Yes, our revenues are bigger than anybody else's, but it we don't run fast and do good things . . ."[15]

PARANOIA 101 WITH PROFESSOR GROVE[16]

Intel Chairman Andy Grove is famously paranoid, a quality he credits with helping to make him one of the most successful corporate leaders of recent times. In his book *Only the Paranoid Survive*, he asserts that change and competitive challenges now develop so quickly that companies have to identify threats to their corporate well-being *before* those threats gather force and blind-side them. Some of the ways to do this are to:

◆ *Identify "strategic inflection points" (SIPs).* Grove defines these as "changes in the business environment so immense that they must be acted upon." The principal way to spot them before they wreak havoc is to adopt the perspective of someone outside your organization who has no vested interest in the status quo.

◆ *Encourage company Cassandras.* From their never-ending stream of nightmare scenarios, genuine causes for concern can be identified.

◆ **Spare the messenger.** Grove says, "It takes many years of consistent conduct to eliminate fear of punishment. . . . It takes only one incident to introduce it."

◆ **Build flexibility into planning.** Companies tend to be too rigid in their planning, Grove writes. Think of planning the same way fire departments must do it: You don't know where the next conflagration will take place, so you shape a flexible team that responds well to unanticipated events. Exxon showed how *not* to do it after the Valdez oil spill; Johnson & Johnson provided the perfect model during the Tylenol bottle-tampering scare.

Grove says it's essential to fight off the thought that business success frees a company from the imperative to stay paranoid. "The more successful you are, the more competition you're going to get. . . . Success brings with it the potential of its own destruction."

HOLD ON TO YOUR EARLY HUNGER

Cisco's purposeful – and thus-far successful – effort to behave like "the biggest startup on the planet" is directed at avoiding the sort of corporate petrification that has so adversely affected other companies that couldn't seem to achieve smashing success without also getting dumb and smug. "What got IBM and Wang in trouble," says John Chambers of his former employers, "was that they did not have competitors for long periods of time, and that unseats you."[17] Unseats, as in removing the impetus to make sure the market wants what you think it wants. "[M]anagement did not make the changes that needed to be made as the market evolved. So our customers told us what we had to do product-wise. They told us we were getting too far away from them, but we just didn't listen. If you're not looking externally, you're looking internally and you're doing politics."[18]

Perhaps no large corporation has so completely failed to look externally in the last half of the 20th century as General Motors – as vividly illustrated by the saga of the redesigned 1991 Chevrolet Caprice. Numerous press accounts noted the design staff's rejection of negative comments on the prototype redesign, such as this one in *The Washington Post*: "[T]he design staff . . . had a reputation for being resentful of marketers, engineers, and other corporate outsiders who had the gumption to tell them what was and was not attractive." When a focus group known as a customer clinic also voiced its strong objections to the proposed new Caprice exterior, design staff VP Charles M. Jordon "didn't like the clinic's reaction. 'We were excited about the design,' he said. 'We decided not to do anything about it. We believed in the design. . . . All the car guys liked the design.'" Caprice sales for 1991 amounted to half the anticipated volume. In 1995, the model was discontinued.[19]

Chambers is apparently right to be concerned that his high-energy, high-tech firm could be infected with the sort of thinking that afflicted GM, IBM, and other corporate behemoths. *Fortune* magazine was moved to sound this alert on examining Microsoft and Intel: "The Internet is beginning to show that they, like IBM and DEC before them, are mortals like everyone else."[20]

A huge plus Chambers has going for him is the seemingly simple ability – but apparently elusive to many other company chiefs – to recognize that others could come along and do unto Cisco as Cisco has done unto still others. "Our biggest competitor two years ago was 20 percent bigger than us," he told *Time* magazine in 1997. "Today we're 300 percent bigger than them. Anyone who thinks that can't happen to them is wrong."[21]

"Everybody naturally resists change. I do as well, and yet we're trying to build a company that thrives on change."

Chambers seems more than a little troubled by the possibility of losing an essential spark while vanquishing all competitors. "Unless you have competition and unless people gear to survival, they don't move rapidly," he says, explaining

> Everybody naturally resists change. I do as well, and yet we're trying to build a company that thrives on change. How do you build it into the culture? What's caused the financial industry to change or the retail industry to adopt e-commerce so quickly or the service providers to adopt the IT infrastructure is competition and survival, and nothing causes a change of behavior like those two.[22]

If you "build it into the culture" by incessantly worrying out loud about it – keeping your troops ever alert to losing their competitive fire – then Cisco already has it.

HOW TO KEEP GROWTH FROM DOUSING COMPETITIVE FIRE[23]

"Creating a successful service operation is unquestionably a difficult task," writes Texas A&M services marketing professor Leonard L. Berry. "However, sustaining success can be even more difficult." In his book *Discovering the Soul of Service*, Berry finds "three specific challenges in sustaining success":

◆ *Operating effectively while growing rapidly.* "Relaxing standards is common when fast-growing companies select, orient, train, and educate many new managers and employees," Berry observes. That's what happened to ValuJet, which Berry says was "deeply troubled . . . well before its tragic May 11, 1996, crash."

◆ *Operating effectively when competing on price.* Berry says that managers of local telephone companies failed to understand the difference between price and value when they cut back on employees and service in the mid-1990s. "Price is price; value is the total experience. . . . Without a superior total experience to offer customers, a company has few, if any, nonpricing options when key competitors cut their prices."

◆ *Retaining the entrepreneurial spirit of the younger, smaller company.* Both corporate and personal entrepreneurship are jeopardized as firms grow, Berry contends. "Rules replace informality . . . turfism replaces teamwork . . . supervisory layers replace impromptu visits." A once "feisty, innovative" Holiday Inn suffered such a fate: "The founder's vision and entrepreneurial spirit faded away."

TAKE THE CALCULATED RISK

Neither a company nor its people can ever afford to stand still, if for no other reason than that its customers' needs will never stand still. Yet too many companies do little more than pay lip service to encouraging employee risk-taking, while heaping various forms of disapproval on any who dare take a risk that fails. "Anyone who takes risks and does not make mistakes is kidding themselves – you're not

> "Anyone who takes risks and does not make mistakes is kidding themselves – you're not taking a risk."

taking a risk," John Chambers says. "And companies who say [they're] risk takers and then you ask their key employees, 'What happens if you miss?' and they say, 'I get shot' – [those companies] aren't risk takers either."[24]

The imperative to boldly go where your company has never gone before is explained this way by Oracle Corp. CEO Lawrence J. Ellison:

> Just as surely as IBM is no longer the center of the universe, they never lost their monopoly on mainframes. It's just that mainframes ceased to be at the center of the universe. The same thing's happening to Intel and Microsoft and the PC now. And they're finding that it's definitely more complicated when customers have a choice and you have to compete. In fact, it's a bitch. You need to build multiple products, and hedge your bets, and sometimes someone beats you.[25]

Ellison's statement is probably precisely on target as an explanation of Cisco's unhesitating plunge into the battle with bigger, more established rivals to provide the "converged" data, voice, and video-transmitting telecommunications systems that telephone companies and other service providers are only starting to purchase. Cisco is in the highly unaccustomed position of holding a minuscule market share in sales of networking gear to phone companies, and is working against decades-long relationships of those companies with first-rate competitors Lucent and Nortel, among others. But the risk to Cisco – and to Chambers personally – of potentially losing sales and, not incidentally, some of its carefully nurtured corporate luster is not just acceptable, but probably essential to its long-term survival.

"Informed and balanced risk-taking" is a skill that companies must develop in their people, say Arthur D. Little consultants

Ronald S. Jonash and Tom Sommerlatte, in their book *The Innovation Premium.* Such companies won't penalize their people:

> . . . for daring to color outside the lines – even when the finished prduct ends up in the wastebasket. . . . Whereas the traditional managerial focus on business systems deadened the confidence and ability that people needed in order to take risks, innovative companies focus on building up those traits and teaching employees how to take the smart risks, informed and balanced gambles that produce a payoff for the company.[26]

Cisco's payoffs from risk-taking have rewarded the company with one of the world's largest market capitalizations. But those risks are all past now, and new ones will determine whether the company's great success can be extended.

DEALING WITH DECONSTRUCTION[27]

John Chambers' continuing determination to mold Cisco for ongoing success in what he calls the "new economy" appears to position the company well for dealing with the "deconstruction" being ushered in by that economy. Deconstruction, according to Boston Consulting Group VPs Philip Evans and Thomas S. Wurster, "presents a dizzying degree of fluidity, indeterminacy, and instability."

In their book *Blown to Bits: How the New Economics of Information Transforms Strategy,* Evans and Wurster say that deconstruction is a process of transformation that essentially "blows up" truths of the nature of commerce that have stood for centuries. It results from the universal connectivity and open standards being ushered in by the information revolution, and brings with it a set of new truths, including these:

◆ No business leader today can presume that the business definitions in his or her business will still be valid a few years from now.

◆ Deconstruction is most likely to strike in precisely those parts of the business where incumbents have most to lose and are least willing to recognize it.

◆ Waiting for someone else to demonstrate the feasibility of deconstruction hands over the biggest advantage a competitor could possibly wish for: time.

◆ The value of winning will escalate, as will the cost of losing.

◆ The hardest step for an incumbent organization is the mental one of seeing the business through a different, deconstructed lens and then acting on this insight.

◆ The subtler pitfall is co-option and passive resistance by a skeptical and self-preserving organization.

◆ Strategy has to be generally but not specifically right, as long as the organization maintains a capacity to learn from its mistakes.

◆ The value of incumbents' best assets is all too often destroyed by the baggage they insist on bringing to the new venture. It is essential at some point to junk your legacy organizations, legacy mindsets, and legacy competencies.

◆ Incumbents can be insurgents, if they choose. They can take some capability of theirs right into the heart of somebody else's business and blow it up.

CHANGE YOUR MINDSET TO EXPECT
SPEEDIER CHANGE

We all know – and perhaps count ourselves among – the computer buyers who wait endlessly to make their next purchase, "Just until the next wave of upgrades is over." Similarly, company leaders may be waiting to align their corporate cultures, customer offerings, sales channels, and marketing with realities of the Digital Age, "Just as soon as the current wave of change is over."

Indications are the wave not only won't end, but will intensify:

◆ "The Internet industry actually is accelerating and the opportunities for winners and losers will sort out much quicker." – John Chambers[28]

◆ "Here in Silicon Valley, ground zero of the new economy, it's clear that this dizzying process of change is just beginning. What lies ahead is an acceleration of the virtuous cycle we've been experiencing" – *Washington Post*[29]

◆ "Strategic blunders and oversights by management have pulled down such powerful and mighty giants as AT&T, Eastman Kodak, and General Motors. Yet there is a less visible but even more critical danger: the inability to adapt to the speed and turbulence of technological change. After massive high-tech investments, management is only beginning to make the organizational changes needed to transform information technology into the potent competitive weapon that it will need to be in the 21st century." – *Business Week*[30]

One might suppose that the task of adjusting individual mindsets and corporate cultures to the dramatic effects of continuous change would be easiest for firms, such as Cisco, that are helping to bring continuous change. But even Internet firms can fall short in accommodating change, according to the story of Netscape related in *Competing on Internet Time* by

Michael Cusumano and David B. Yoffie. "Netscape was second to none in its ability to take a set of short-term ideas, turn them into products, and run like hell," they write. However,

> . . . when it came to strategic planning, long-term often meant a fiscal quarter or, at most, a year. . . . In sharp contrast [to] archrival Microsoft, Netscape managers eschewed multi-year plans. . . . The advantage of Microsoft's approach to strategic planning was the fact that the company had a structure in place to look systematically at its environment and then develop a set of plans both to react to that environment and to try to shape it.[31]

> "Every industry is in transition. Every country is in transition. The Internet will wait for no one. Not any individual. Not any company. Not any country."

Neither will companies outside the Internet realm find refuge from the vortex of continuous change. John Chambers says, "Companies that don't [attempt to overhaul] over the next decade will be at a competitive disadvantage. It's no longer just a high-tech phenomenon. Every industry is in transition. Every country is in transition. The Internet will wait for no one. Not any individual. Not any company. Not any country."[32]

FIGHT COMPLACENCY THAT CAN ACCOMPANY SUCCESS

Thanks to his disturbing experiences at IBM and Wang, John Chambers is as aware as any CEO of the threats to corporate success entailed in having achieved success. So he never tires of impressing upon everyone at Cisco – including himself – the tenets of maintaining a company's competitive edge:

◆ *Remember past success – is past.* Too many companies have allowed records of success to go to their collective heads, seeming to think that past accomplishments ensured ongoing success. Remember that corporate history is littered with evidence of the opposite: Success can breed the arrogance that leads to downfall.

◆ *Make experience your favorite teacher.* Although he would hardly have viewed it as such at the time, John Chambers' then-unwelcome experience at IBM and Wang probably instilled in him the proper caution and wariness for handling Cisco's phenomenal success in the 1990s. Make lemonade from the lemons in your career by learning lessons from the school of hard knocks.

◆ *Embrace paranoia.* There's nothing pathologic in thinking people are out to get you when people *are* out to get you. With the intensity and uncertainties of today's global competition, you may do your firm a favor by believing it could all come tumbling down in the blink of an eye.

◆ *Hold on to your early hunger.* It's tough to maintain entrepreneurial energy when your company has soared to success. Find ways to keep the spirit alive, such as Cisco's conscious effort to adopt features of the cultures of companies it acquires.

◆ *Take the calculated risk.* John Chambers says the company that doesn't tolerate failure doesn't take any risks and, therefore, doesn't change with the times. So you must not merely tolerate failure, but encourage it. Responsible risk is the only route to sustained success.

◆ *Change your mindset to expect speedier change.* Waiting for the pace of change to ease is a fool's game; change may be today's only constant for managers. The challenge is to anticipate where change is taking you, and be ready when you get there.

NOTES

1. Jones, Del, and Belton, Beth, "Cisco Chief: Virtual Close to Hit Big," *USA Today*, 12 October 1999.

2. Wheelwright, Geoffrey, "The Problems of Survival in the New Digital World," *Financial Times*, 1 September 1999.

3. Holson, Laura M., "Cisco Systems to Invest $1 Billion in the Accounting Giant KPMG," *New York Times*, 8 August 1999.

4. Chung, David, "Internet Investors Can Learn from Lessons of Early '90s," *Investor's Business Daily*, 11 August 1999.

5. Rodin, Robert, *Free, Perfect, and Now*, Simon & Schuster, New York, 1999.

6. Slater, Robert, *Saving Big Blue: Leadership Lessons & Turnaround Tactics of IBM's Lou Gerstner*, McGraw-Hill, New York, 1999.

7. Cave, Andrew, "The Cisco Kid Grows Up to Be Mr. Internet," *Daily Telegraph*, 9 October 1999.

8. ABC-TV, "20/20," 15 September 1999.

9. Cave, Andrew, "The Cisco Kid Grows Up to Be Mr. Internet," *Daily Telegraph*, 9 October 1999.

10. Author interview.

11. Author interview.

12. Laplante, Alice, "The Man Behind Cisco," *Electronic Business*, December 1997.

13. Baum, Geoff, "Cisco's CEO," *Forbes*, 23 February 1998.

14. CNBC Network, "Business Center," 6 February 1998.

15. Wallace, James, and Erickson, Jim, *Hard Drive: Bill Gates and the Making of the Microsoft Empire*, HarperBusiness, New York, 1992.

16. Grove, Andy, *Only the Paranoid Survive*, Currency-Doubleday, New York, 1996.

17. Medford, Cassimir, "Unleashing the Internet Economy," *VAR-Business*, 16 November 1998.

18. Daly, James, "The Art of the Deal," *Business 2.0*, October 1999.

19. Swoboda, Frank, "GM Misses Mark with Bulky Caprice," *Washington Post*, 6 July 1992.

20. Schlender, Brent, "The Real Road Ahead," *Fortune*, 25 October 1999.

21. Ramo, Joshua Cooper, "Cisco Guards the Gate," *Time*, 9 June 1997.

22. Daly, James, "The Art of the Deal," *Business 2.0*, October 1999.

23. Berry, Leonard L., *Discovering the Soul of Service: The Nine Drivers of Sustainable Business Success*, Free Press, New York, 1999.

24. Daly, James, "The Art of the Deal," *Business 2.0*, October 1999.

25. Schlender, Brent, "The Real Road Ahead," *Fortune*, 25 October 1999.

26. Jonash, Ronald S., and Sommerlatte, Tom, *The Innovation Premium*, Perseus, Cambridge, Massachusetts, 1999.

27. Evans, Philip, and Wurster, Thomas S., *Blown to Bits: How the New Economics of Information Transforms Strategy*, Harvard Business School Press, Boston, 2000.

28. CNNfn, "Market Coverage," 26 August 1999.

29. Ignatius, David, "Online in the New Economy," *Washington Post*, 11 July 1999.

30. Byrne, John, "The Corporation of the Future," *Business Week*, 24 August 1998.

31. Cusumano, Michael, and Yoffie, David B., *Competing on Internet Time*, Free Press, New York, 1998.

32. Jones, Del, and Belton, Beth, "Cisco Chief: Virtual Close to Hit Big," *USA Today*, 12 October 1999.

HOW TO SUCCEED THE CISCO WAY

Cisco's market capitalization makes it the fifth-largest company in the world – after only 15 years of existence. In the decade since the company went public, it's stock appreciated by more than 65,000 percent – the third-highest increase in the US during the 1990s.

How has the company achieved such remarkable results? A thorough examination of the considerable reporting on the firm since its inception points to the 10 secrets of success described in preceding pages. They're listed again here, with the essence of their explanation to guide you in taking your business to Cisco-like heights:

1. MAKE YOUR PASSION YOUR BUSINESS – PREACH IT ALWAYS EVERYWHERE

With today's pervasive global competition and continual change, it takes more than a desire for corporate and personal success in material terms to win over the long term. You and your organization have got to be dedicated to your cause – a visceral belief that your offerings add something of unique value to customers' lives. John Chambers and his team clearly hold such a belief about the role Cisco plays in bringing the instant global communicating power of the Internet to everyone.

2. WIN THE WORLD WITH E-COMMERCE

Your company, like others, may gain much from exploiting the capabilities of online sales. But as Cisco has dramatically demonstrated, additional sales are but the tip of the e-commerce iceberg. The Internet provides unprecedented opportunities for growing your sales and revenue while lowering unit costs of production and servicing. Your company can win big by seizing these opportunities before – or better than – its competitors.

3. USE THE NET TO REVOLUTIONIZE INTERNAL OPERATIONS

The Internet's advantages don't just apply in the world beyond your company's doors – look inward to transform entire categories of corporate operations. You can follow Cisco's lead to accomplish more while spending less in areas such as performance reports and analysis, staff recruiting, employee training, and knowledge sharing.

4. PUT PEOPLE BEFORE PRODUCTS, PROFITS, AND EVERYTHING ELSE

John Chambers understands the increasingly decisive competitive advantage in having employees who outperform competitors' workers. As traditional differences between competitors – such as product quality and customer service – gradually disappear, workforce quality assumes ever-greater importance. To get and keep the best people, great pay and perks are still essential but insufficient; intangibles such as challenging work are also required.

5. LISTEN CONSTANTLY TO CUSTOMERS

Cisco is a paragon of customer focus, to the extent that the company has made two acquisitions suggested by customers. John Chambers doesn't rely on subordinates to keep him apprised of what customers want; he spends half his time in direct contact with customers. Customer focus may sound lofty, but Cisco demonstrates that it's composed of everyday, nitty-gritty attention to learning what customers need right now and delivering solutions in the blink of an eye.

6. SERVE YOUR CORE CUSTOMERS FROM START TO END-TO-END

Customer needs are dynamic, changing faster and more frequently than ever before. Cisco is built to respond in kind, with a horizontal structure that keeps the company agile enough to give customers what they want when they want it. It's a model that will increasingly be required for corporate survival in the 21st century.

7. LOOK TO LEAD IN EVERY LINE OF BUSINESS

Some commentators say market share is passe, but it's hard to argue that the stunning, sustained success of companies that pursue it – Cisco and GE, for example – is somehow not genuine or meaningful to stakeholders. Follow the lead of smart CEOs, such as John Chambers and Jack Welch: Place market leadership in its proper context – as *a* measure, not *the* measure of corporate success – and proceed to achieve it in every line of business.

8. BUY RIGHT TO GROW LIKE GANGBUSTERS

Corporate acquisition is an art practiced by many firms that fail miserably – which is why Cisco's buyouts are amazing in both their number and eventual success. Make buyouts work by insisting they meet rigid criteria, making everyone involved a winner, and delivering on commitments after the sale.

9. IF YOU DON'T BUY 'EM, JOIN 'EM

Internal growth sufficient to meet customer and investor expectations is increasingly a challenge for many companies. Smart firms like Cisco are increasingly looking to strategic partnerships as a key mechanism to keep growing. Alliances require commitment and hard work, but can pay off big in extending your company's reach to new technologies, markets, and customers.

10. RESIST COMPLACENCY THAT CAN ACCOMPANY SUCCESS

Oh, how the corporate mighty have fallen, including two – IBM and Wang – while John Chambers was along for the ride. In retrospect, he couldn't have been more fortunate; the experiences prepared him to handle soaring success at Cisco with appropriate caution and wariness. Your best course, like his, may be to acknowledge the vagaries of modern competition – and steel your firm against the downfall that may await the company at every turn.

LAST WORD: WHITHER CISCO, THE INTERNET, AND YOU?

Not everyone shares John Chambers' view of the Internet as the agent of transformation of the world economy, the spark that has triggered a "second Industrial Revolution." One such skeptic is marketing and advertising executive Gerry Griffin. In his book entitled *.Con*, he likens the rise of the dot-com companies to the 19th century California gold rush:

> If the commentators are to be believed, the e-gold rush is sweeping the world, blazing a dramatic and unstoppable path through traditional commercial practice and thinking. . . . Take away the techno-babble and the hype, and there is often little mystery to what is happening . . . there are two key themes. First, ordinary business people can utilize the Internet and electronic commerce in all their technological finery. . . . Second, booms have an unhappy history of coming to abrupt ends. . . . All who ride on the wave of hyperbole risk a substantial fall.[1]

A similar, although less ominous, view of the future is rendered by securities firm president Edward Wedbush, who says,

> Ultimately, I think the Internet will be looked upon as another communications system, somewhat like telephone lines and

electricity. Electricity flows from one spot to the other and people don't think about electricity. They think about the appliances at either end of the system.[2]

Should that come to pass, Cisco Systems may settle into a comfortable middle age as the 21st century version of the old AT&T – Ma Bell. Its stock may become a favorite of "widows & orphans" – those who seek only a solid dividend and little downside risk.

In a world where the information revolution helped bring the collapse of totalitarian governments and ushered in global competition, it's unlikely that any company can long survive as a ponderous, unchallenged monopolist of the AT&T ilk.

But the mere mention of such a scenario highlights its unlikelihood. In a world where the information revolution helped bring the collapse of totalitarian governments and ushered in global competition, it's unlikely that any company can long survive as a ponderous, unchallenged monopolist of the AT&T ilk.

Far more likely is the potential that Cisco and other firms – in high-tech or not – will be forced by creative, energetic upstarts to find ways of being even more agile and intelligent than they are today.

As Cisco's advertising asks: "Are you ready?"

NOTES

1. Griffin, Gerry, .Con, Suntop Media, London, 1999.

2. Chung, David, "Internet Investors Can Learn from Lessons of Early '90s," *Investor's Business Daily*, 11 August 1999.

INDEX